CATS FIND YOU

—◆—

HOPE, HAPPINESS, AND A CAT CALLED STICKY

CHUCK HAWLEY WITH NADYA SIAPIN

CONTENTS

— • —

INTRODUCTION/FOREWORD

I ntroduction
When we started writing this book, I wasn't quite sure what it was going to be about. I knew I wasn't the story, but there is a wonderful story here. The lessons I have learned from this strange cat fame journey are just too good not to share. When I found Sticky, the world was an angry place. It was such an angry place that multiple cars sped right over a kitten on a roadway on an early Friday morning, without even slowing down. When I stopped for the kitten, people suddenly slowed down but it was to yell at me to get off the road, not to help the kitten. Even worse, someone had found the time to cover that kitten in glue and put him on that road in the first place. That is how angry the world was on that early October, Friday morning.

I felt that anger and angst in our world, just like everyone else did. Every day, it was on the news. It was spray painted on the walls I saw on my way to work. It even flew from flags on the back of pick-up trucks. It seemed there was a lot to be angry about. And then I came across this kitten. Something so helpless and maybe even a product of that angry time we were living in, that just needed some help. I couldn't know how that kitten would change my life or the amazing things it would show me that morning I stopped for him. I just knew he needed some help, and that is what we are supposed to do. Help each other out when we can. The world had just forgotten that for a moment. It took a magical kitten to remind me and people all around the world that kindness... always wins. And then I realized... that is what the story was about. Kindness.

But it wasn't just that. This entire experience has taught me we are all someone with an ability to make a change in the world. As we were writing this book, I was reminded of how I used to wish for some kind of life-changing event that would force me to appreciate life the way I saw some folks savor every minute of their own. Man, did I get it. But those life changing moments are around us every day. I just never realized it. Through many years of day to day struggles, I never took the time to notice the changes we all make in people's lives every day or even allow myself to believe I was the kind of someone that could make those changes. I always was. And you are too. Kindness is how you change lives. Kindness is how you become someone. There was a very controversial radio host that passed away the year this book was written. He was mean and cruel and somehow had a huge following. It was pointed out to me that no one speaks about him anymore. You never hear his name, just months after his death. I hear Mr. Rogers' name at least once a month without ever even trying. I think my point is proven right there. Kindness always wins.

This story is also about angels. I'm not a particularly religious man, but I do believe in angels. I believe in them because I have been fortunate enough to take shelter under the wings of some folks who could have been nothing other than angels. Without them and their kindness, I may have had a very different story. Most of them didn't even know they were saving me at the time. I think we all have the ability to be an angel to someone at some point, and there is a good chance you are someone's angel right now and don't even know it. I know this little cat has been referred to as an angel more times than I ever have, and who knows... he just might be.

There are a lot of cat books out there, with amazing stories of their own. While Sticky's story is a cat story, it is so much more. This one kitten is responsible for more acts of kindness and just plain goodness than any human, I personally know. He has saved lives, changed lives, and even been the comfort at the end of lives. He definitely changed my life and I think his story may just change a few more before it is through. If this one little kitten, that someone deemed disposable enough to cover in glue and put on a road, can do all of this, imagine what you can do.

"If you get a chance, take it. If it changes your life, let it."

Let me tell you a little story friends...

1

MEET CHUCK

Meet Chuck/BS (Before Sticky)

On a cool, fall day in 1986, my mother and I stepped out of a concrete stairway and onto the platform of a busy commuter train station in Yokosuka, Japan. We were living there at the time with my Navy Chaplain stepfather.

As Americans in Japan, we were used to standing out. However, besides being two of the very few Americans on the platform, my face was on every poster around the station. Walking past the newsstand in the center of the platform, I grinned, seeing my face on two of the magazines there as well.

As my Mom kept pointing out the various posters, holding my arm and smiling, the station buzzed. As we boarded our train with the other waiting passengers, my face was on every poster in there, as well.

Once onboard the packed train, all the way to our destination, I signed autographs while my mom looked on with surprise, pride, and amusement. I couldn't tell you what was being said as these kids shoved magazines, papers, or whatever it was they had for me to sign towards me but there were smiles, pats... even a few tears.

It's a heady thing for a fatherless boy who'd always felt less than everyone around him, and I have no real idea how I ended up in that moment. I'd certainly never intended to be a model, but I'd finally found my place in this world. I was a famous model.

I was someone.

Well, except...

When I say my early life was complicated, it's almost impossible even for me to make sense of it. My mom is my mom, but she didn't fully raise me. She had me just after turning sixteen, after being already married and divorced to an equally young father I would never know. She was just a kid herself. In my early years, I was partially raised by my grandma, right next to my mom, aunt, and uncle. My uncle is only a couple of years older than me, which always made him more of a brother to me than an uncle. My first memories are from around 3 years old but they aren't from my grandma's house. My Mom had gotten remarried and, as I have been told, moved us to Austin, Texas. The common denominator in these memories is confusion, but in the quiet way, you're confused when you're very young.

My very first memory is sliding down a snowy hill, sitting in an empty, white clothes basket. My mom was always good at making something out of nothing. My second memory then would be waking up one night and walking through the apartment, everyone else asleep. Half empty drinks were scattered all around. People had been here, and now they weren't.

The third is of a gun laying on a wooden table and the fourth is my Mom holding my hand, leading me to the front door. There are one or two police officers in this memory, although I can't quite place why, and I don't know where my stepdad is or why we were leaving.

And suddenly, we're on a Greyhound bus. It's dark outside. I can't really see out because I'm sitting in the aisle seat. Fidgeting in my seat, I stare around at all the adults, some of them sleeping in their own seats. I know we're still in Texas, but where are we going? Back to Grandma's? I don't know what's happening.

Towards the front of the bus, a lady gets up, walking down the aisle towards me. I can't see her face, she's just a silhouette. The lights shone behind her, and I stared up at her. She looks like an angel.

I don't know why or what she saw on my face, but she paused next to me, bending to put her hand on my head, resting it there gently. "It's gonna be okay," she whispered and smiled before she continued down the aisle.

I sighed, relaxing. That one moment of reassurance changed everything. Suddenly, I felt everything really would be okay. This beautiful woman, my angel, said it would be, and that was enough.

It sounds like a country song, but she became known as my 'Greyhound Angel' when I would talk about her later in my life. The person I thought of whenever I saw an opportunity to maybe help someone out, and especially a child. Her kindness meant the world to a scared kid. That one brief moment of kindness has been the catalyst for more acts of kindness by me than I can even tell you. I'm sure she forgot about me as soon as she passed me by, but I have never forgotten her.

We ended up going back to Grandma's house, and then came one round after another of mom getting her life sorted, getting an apartment, then I'd go live with her. Sometimes it was for a couple of weeks, other times it was only for a few days. Then things would fall apart, and I'd be back with Grandma and Grandpa.

In those days, my living situation—teenage mom and no dad—was semi unconventional, and when you're in that situation, through no fault of your own, you feel like there's something wrong with you. I'd go to school, hear other kids talking about their dads, see them at ball games, cheering their kids on, and I knew I was missing out.

I felt inferior, this little kid in the corner, watching everyone else have families while I bounced around from place to place. I couldn't even comprehend the differences between my life and that of the other kids. I'd watch them, wondering what it would be like to have that support, but at the same time, it wasn't something I could really imagine.

It seemed to me that if I felt like, 'no one'–then they must feel like, 'someone'. I knew that must be a feeling, but I couldn't have even begun to tell you what that felt like.

I was a painfully shy and very insecure child, but I did my best not to show it, walking into every new school like I owned it. As if it had no secrets from me and I knew everything about everyone. And I kind of did, or I at least knew enough. I learned to read people quickly and developed a sense of who someone was almost before we even spoke. I suppose it's a survival skill for a child in the position I was in, but I learned the easiest way to get along was to be liked, at least a little, by every group. Sometimes it worked. Sometimes it did not.

By the time I graduated, I'd gone to fourteen schools in twelve years. My last 2 years were at the same school, so you can see how much I moved around. Life became a series of temporary situations at a very young age.

Things changed drastically when Grandpa died. I was eight, almost nine, and living with my mom and her boyfriend at the time. It was sudden, a heart attack, and he was far too young, only fifty-one. In that moment, I lost the closest thing I'd ever had to a dad. We all did.

Different circumstances, from lack of Life Insurance to my grandma's lack of job skills, led us all to move to Hawaii, where my aunt had moved the previous year.

My mom had a boyfriend stationed there, a pilot in the Navy named Mike. My mother left before the rest of us, getting married shortly before my grandmother, uncle, and my arrival on the island. I remember the smells of the jet fuel mixed with the faint smell of flowers and humid Hawaiian air and the warm breeze blowing down the corridor of the outside hallways of the Honolulu airport. We had left everything we had ever known behind in Texas, so stepping off of that plane was literally stepping into the beginning of a completely new and different life. And I wasn't sad about it.

I suddenly had a dad like everyone else did. He was there as much as he could be, playing catch with me and, from what I remember, smiling every single time he saw me. We went to the movies a lot and I remember a lot of bowling. When my bike was stolen, I tried my hardest not to cry. He pulled me into him, squeezing me, saying, "It's OK buddy, I'd cry too." I remember a lot of little moments like that. He was a good guy. Looking back as an adult now, what I see is a very kind man who was doing his best to fill in as a dad to a kid who he knew just needed to feel like some kind of father figure loved him. I did feel like he loved me and I loved him very much.

Of course, I had a different relationship than my mom did with Mike, and it wasn't long before he and mom started having problems. They decided the responsible thing to do was to go to the base chaplain for counseling sessions. Let's just say that counseling didn't work out, because about the time I was turning ten, mom was divorcing Mike, and the chaplain was divorcing his wife and leaving his family of twenty something years, to marry my mom, who was still only in her mid-twenties.

He was almost twice her age.

So my mom and stepdad's counselor, a chaplain in the navy, somehow talked my mom into leaving her husband and the first 'dad' I had ever had, and became her new husband, and my next 'dad'.

I don't hold this against my mom. If I'm honest, I did for a long time. But as time has gone on, I have realized she was just one of many in this guys long line of victims. This is how this chaplain operated and my mom was a young, beautiful and easy target.

You know how kids can see the truth of situations? I saw who he was right away, but my mom thought he loved her. He convinced her she was special to him. He even adopted me, and they changed my last name to his, but despite this, we would never be close.

Modeling

As crazy as it sounds to say now, I was pretty famous for a minute in Japan as a teenager in the 1980s. Minimal super-vision, lots of money, and my 'supervisors' sliding me drugs in the background. Those were some of the loneliest times of my life, but at the same time, I held those memories close through most of my adult life because somehow, in that empty fame, I felt like I was someone.

Shortly before I turned sixteen, my mom's new chaplain husband was stationed in Japan. As you do when you're a Navy family in America, we packed up and moved when we were told to. It took a while before we could move on to the Navy base, but fortunately, I could go to the base school right away.

We had moved from Long Beach California, where we had moved when my mom and his respective marriages were ended in Hawaii. There was a backyard wedding in a rental house in Garden Grove and just like that, we were supposed to be a family. I don't think his predatory behavior towards women had stopped just because he had married my mom. It may have slowed down a bit, but I think this behavior was all becoming more and more apparent as we left California and headed to Japan.

My mom was beginning to get caught up in all of those heartaches and drama as we arrived in Yokosuka and I was already 3 or 4 years into not liking my new step father by this point. I don't know that I knew what exactly was going on in his and my mom's relationship, but I knew it never felt good and I just wanted to escape home.

As life had taught me to do by that point, I made friends pretty quickly in Japan with a group of kids my age who already lived on base and I even had my first girlfriend, Autumn. One night as I did as often as I could in those days, and anywhere I could really, I spent the night at one of those friends, Scott's house. The next day my entire world changed and for years and years to come, although I wouldn't know it until a couple weeks later.

In the morning, right after breakfast, Scott's mom started collecting her things. "Chuck, Scott has a photo shoot this morning. Would you like to come?"

A what?

"Modeling. It'll just be for a few hours."

I laughed. Scott modeling? Oh, yeah, I had to go, if only to laugh at him and give him a hard time.

I hung out by the car, watching Scott get his hair done, posing, all of that, while photographers ran around snapping photos by the hundreds. The photographers took photos of everyone there, candid shots that I thought nothing of at the time.

Two weeks later, I'd completely forgotten about it. Mom and I were hanging out in the kitchen when the phone rang. She answered, but I tuned the conversation out until she hung up.

"Chuck?" she walked over to stand in front of me. "Did you go to a modeling tryout a couple weeks ago?"

"No?" I scoffed. "As if I'd do that."

"Well." She sat down across from me. "That was a modeling agency, and they'd like you to do a photo shoot for them."

"What are you talking about?" Nothing about this made any sense, but mom's next words changed everything.

"They said they'll pay you $500 to go to Tokyo and let them take photos of you."

I sat up straight. "Um. Yes. Absolutely. They want to pay me $500?" I don't think I had ever seen $500 at one time, at that point in my life. Especially not my own $500. "They can take all the photos they want."

So, I went to Tokyo for a day. It was half an hour of them cutting my hair, a couple hours of photos, then they handed me the Yen equivalent of $500 and said, "See you later."

Holy crap! Five hundred for that? And I get out of the house?

The next week, there was another call, and then another. I'd be taken to various locations around Japan, paid insane amounts of money for a kid, and all I had to do was my best to stare into the distance or look cool.

Scott and I ended up working together a lot. We came as a pair, and we were popular, gone every weekend, making money, and living it up. Scott was far more responsible than I was, and his version of modeling looked quite a bit different from mine. I think he saved his money. I did not. I don't remember him ever really partaking in the drug side of things. I certainly did. For him, it was an opportunity to make some money. For me, it was an opportunity to escape, and I escaped every chance I got.

When modeling took off, I got less and less supervision at home. Mom was dealing with her increasingly toxic relationship and she just... didn't have time to pay much attention to me. This made all that 'escaping' far easier than it would have been otherwise.

My Navy Chaplain stepfather had found the perfect position from which to practice his predation. The trusted, high-ranking older chaplain, who wooed the women he would counsel into a false sense of security until he could have his way with them, leaving them too ashamed or embarrassed to say anything. Who would believe them over him, anyway? As I would learn later, this happened a lot.

It didn't help anyone's situation that he and I thoroughly disliked each other. I didn't like who he was and I wanted no part of him. He didn't like that I wasn't falling for his lies and persona, and he wanted nothing to do with me. As I was writing this book, I thought about instance after instance of things that I went through with him I can't imagine going through with my kids, two of whom are the same age I am telling you about. I decided on sticking with this... he was just a horrible person. But it was that set of dysfunctional circumstances that allowed me to run wild as a kid in a foreign country.

All the teachers and most of the parents know what's going on in my parents' relationship because everyone knows everyone in what is basically a small American town in a foreign country. And I suppose everyone assumed that someone else was supervising me somewhere. Including my own parents.

The only sort of parental guidance I experienced came from Autumn's mother, Betsy Husser. Autumn and I didn't date for very long, and I feel I should point out this was through no fault of Autumns. I was a jerk. But even after we broke up, they let me continue coming around to their house.

The Hussers were our group's unofficial clubhouse. We were in and out all the time. Betsy always had a snack, a word of advice, or a rebuke when I needed it. She became one of those angels that took me under their wing, and had it not been for her, my life would have turned out much differently.

She stood up for her daughter when necessary and gave me a bit of a scolding when I needed it but she never treated me differently. She never spoke down to me, and she didn't throw me away like so many other adults had.

I always felt like a part of their family. The family I really wanted and needed was half a world away, but Betsy gave me the kindness that held me together just enough to make it through some of the loneliest days of my life. I am eternally grateful for that beautiful soul.

Two months after those first photo shoots, I was at the modeling agency and they called me downstairs. Entering the lobby, people—other teenagers like me—started screaming, holding out magazines, photos, slips of paper. Anything for an autograph.

I had no idea what was going on as my agent ushered me into the small mob of kids, smiling.

"Go on," she said. "Sign them. They came here for you."

And just like that, I felt like somebody. To shoot suddenly from feeling inferior to everyone with a more normal home life to national fame is an amazing feeling and one I treasured for many years after, although I didn't fully understand why until years later.

By the time those kids surrounded me on that train from Yokosuka with my mom, this kind of adoration had almost become commonplace.

For almost a year, I lived the life of a junior rock star. Free drugs, drinking occasionally with Yakuza members at Japanese bars, and many more little 'benefits' that came along with low level, 1980s, Japanese fame.

They once flew me to Okinawa for a photoshoot in a private jet where I was greeted by screaming Japanese kids and spent my first hour just signing autographs. I was driven to a luxury resort where I had a private bungalow and handed a credit card to spend as I pleased. Despite the credit card, someone still gave me a white, furry sweatpants type suit. They even drove me to a runway at an abandoned airport where I could drive the photographer's Porsche as fast as I wanted to.

I 'worked' a grand total of four hours that weekend, the 'work' consisting of riding a horse down a beach and me doing my best version of staring out longingly at the ocean, holding a flag.

They treated me like a star the entire time.

I was sixteen. No rules. No supervision. No guidance. Just a kid running wild in a foreign country.

My mom assumed these people were taking care of me responsibly, but I bought LSD for the first time from one of my chaperones on the way home from that Okinawa trip. Before that, they'd simply hand me cash in an envelope, and there'd usually be a little baggie of something extra.

At home the day after returning from that Okinawa trip, I took that LSD before school. At some point during the day, I left school and just never came back. My mom had found out I had skipped school that day and called me into the kitchen to talk about why I had left. I met her in the kitchen, wearing what was essentially a polar bear costume, still tripping on LSD for the very first time, as I stood in front of her and swore I'd get my act together and do better in school.

And she believed me. Well, I don't know if she believed me, but she accepted it as an answer. There was just that much drama going on in the rest of the house for anyone to even try to pay attention to how far off the rails I was going.

That was the level of supervision and guidance I had at that time in my life. Structure or direction were virtually nonexistent. I had no work ethic. It was terrible for my ego, and even worse for my perception of reality.

But it sure was a great distraction from a home life I wanted no part of.

In the middle of all this fame and fortune, I strangely found myself the loneliest I have ever been in my entire life. It all really showed up one night when I was away for a photoshoot. I think I was in Tokyo but don't really remember. They'd given me a suite high up in this fancy hotel. Drugs and drinks littered the room behind me while I stood at the window, looking out over the city.

This hotel sat at a busy corner, crosswalks everywhere. The light changed, hordes of people crossing, walking with their groups of friends, and I realized I had no one. My parents didn't even know where I was. None of these people cared about me, only what I could do for them.

Reality Check

As suddenly as I rose to fame, it disappeared from my grasp.

Mom finally divorced the chaplain, and he married her best friend, her maid of Honor, from that backyard, California wedding. That's how good this guy was at his game.

Mom decided it was time we went back to the States, and we moved to Sacramento, California, where my grandmother had moved to. I disappeared from Japan without a trace. With no warning, either.

As soon as I could, I headed over to the nearest modeling agency, my portfolio in hand. After all, I'd been insanely popular in Japan. It would be the same In America.

There was no doubt in my mind. I was a model. Period. That was it.

The receptionist looked up at me, her eyebrows raised in astonishment when I announced I was a model and would like to apply.

"Really?" was all she said. Finally, she relented and called a scout down.

He smothered a laugh, looking at my photos, but shook his head. "Listen, kid, you're not a model. You've gotta know how to move, how to look, and how to do it on command. The top models, they go to school for this kind of thing. Now, if you're serious about modeling, we can help you get into school. When you're done, there might even be a job in it for you afterwards."

It quickly became clear that he was more interested in getting me to sign up for expensive classes than ever hiring me to be a model, so I left. I went to another agency and there thcy greeted me with the same lack of interest and after a third and final dismissal from a third and final agency, reality set in. I was no longer a model. I was no longer someone.

As I was realizing I was back to being 'nothing', I watched my friends going off to start their lives in college. There would be no college for me. Instead, my first actual job would be at a sandwich shop, which only lasted until my first paycheck.

Any self confidence I may have gathered up from my time in Japan was quickly being beaten out of me with the realization that back in the States, I was just another face in the crowd. It also hurt when I realized how much I had to work in order to make even a fraction of the money I used to take for granted.

After two weeks, I got my first check. No drugs in the envelope, and doing the math now, I'm guessing it was around $130. I was sure it had to be a mistake. How could that be correct? I went and explained to the 20-year-old-ish woman that was my manager at the time that my check was clearly wrong.

After doing some calculations on her desk calculator, she turned to me. "No, that is correct," she assured me.

I attempted again to argue my case, explaining that I had worked FIFTY hours on that check, so clearly... this could not be correct. At that point, this bewildered woman asked me how much I thought I made. I responded I had no idea how much I made and that I just knew I'd worked fifty hours making sandwiches. There was no way this check was correct.

"You make $3.37 an hour," was her response.

"Only $3.37 every HOUR?!" I shot back. "What the hell? Who would do this for $3.37 an hour? Who?!"

"You are," she replied.

I stared at her, stunned. My manager was just as surprised at my reaction as I was at the amount I made. I'm sure she wondered why this kid thought he should be paid more, but I was reminded all over again of who I was.

Nobody. A fatherless kid with no direction and no real prospects.

Grandma always believed in me, yes. Even when no one else did, she constantly told me I was a star in her eyes. She also had a different take on my time in Japan and modeling fame than most. "I'm glad that ended," she'd say. "That fame had to leave or else you'd have been a mess. We might not have gotten you back."

Looking at it now, she was right.

"Don't worry," she always added. "You'll be famous again someday, Charlie. Then you'll know what to do with it." I had no idea what she meant by that, but she never lied to me, so maybe....

Grandma always had the best but most simple advice. One time, as I went on about some woe or another I had gotten myself into, she stared at me, patiently listened. When I was done telling her my story, probably unaware of the role my own actions had played in getting me into this situation, she took my face in her tiny, soft hands. She looked me right in the eyes and said, "You know you don't have to do *everything* the hard way, Charlie?" Then she kissed me on the forehead and walked away. Advice like that. Short on words and long in lesson.

She was also the kindest person I'd ever known, and I'd always wanted to be just like her. She suffered from her own lack of self-confidence and I don't know if she ever really realized just how cool she was, but she was the best thing that ever happened to me. All I ever wanted to do was make her proud, and she constantly let me know how proud she was of me. Even when I didn't feel like there was much to be proud of. I like to say it only takes one person to make a difference in someone's life, but I was lucky enough to have a few. Grandma and Betsy Husser were the two people in my early life that I just never wanted to disappoint and both made an enormous difference.

It's funny, looking at it now. Betsy had been a part of my life for such a short time, and it took twenty-five years before I would speak to her again. But all those years in between? I lived my life the way I did so that I wouldn't disappoint a woman who'd given me family, kindness, and a sense of belonging when I had none, and who I thought I may never even see or speak to again. THAT is the power of kindness and a great example of how it can change a person's life.

In California, I only had Grandma's reassurances that I was someone, even without the fame and fortune, but at least I could easily see my best friend and biggest support again.

One evening, when I was seventeen, Mom found me at home. She didn't hold back, hem and haw, or stutter. She just said, "We're moving to Texas."

"Why?" I recoiled. I didn't want to go to Texas. I had a girlfriend and friends here, some of whom I'd known in Japan. While I didn't care for the jobs available, I doubted Texas had anything better.

"I'm getting married," Mom replied. "So, we're moving to Abilene, Texas."

I snorted. "No way. Good luck to you, but I'm staying here."

Something on my face must have told her I meant it, because she didn't try very hard to change my mind.

Instead, I decided to move to Hawaii, to Kauai, to be exact. My friends from Japan went with me, and my girlfriend, Gail, followed a month or so later.

I was seventeen, and I went to party and be a surfer. I had no desire to do much more than have fun and enjoy my life. Gail came over with a white picket fence on her mind. Since our views were so different, our relationship lasted barely two months—just long enough to celebrate my eighteenth birthday—before she decided to move back to California.

I flew back with her to help her move; the breakup being mostly friendly. A few days before I was set to catch my flight back to Hawaii, however, she calls and tells me she's pregnant.

I'd been with Grandma when she called. Stunned—shocked—I hung up, staring at Grandma blankly. "Gail's pregnant," I heard myself say, as if from a distance.

She watched me, her eyes shrewd. "Well, then. You're not going back to Hawaii."

I shook my head, sure I hadn't heard her right. "What? Why not?"

"Because you're having a baby," she said patiently, love and exasperation in her eyes.

"Wait a minute," I said, struggling to process her words. "You're saying I can't go back? But...that doesn't make sense."

It didn't really sink in. In my life, in my world, there was absolutely no need to stick around. You split. That's the way the world works.

But, over the next few days, my perspective completely shifted from 'you can split without guilt' to 'there is no way you can never split.'

The more I thought about my coming child, the more it reminded me of my own life and circumstances. How small and like nothing I had felt throughout childhood.

How I still felt.

I realized I couldn't do that to my own kid. I had to be there for it, and I would. I promised myself I'd be there for that baby, loving the child and ensuring they never grew up without a father's love.

I'd be sure to be for my kid, what I hadn't had.

The Struggling Years

While I'd already decided to be there for my kid, I still hadn't expected marriage. I could be there for the kid without marrying Gail, but according to my friends and family, I couldn't.

In the end, I was so far removed from the wedding and the planning that on the morning of our wedding, sick after drinking so much at my bachelor party I had given myself alcohol poisoning, that I had to call her to find out which church to go to.

I so badly didn't want to marry her. I didn't want to marry anyone. I just knew I wasn't ready for a commitment like that, and in my experience, marriage just didn't end well.

I repeated it, over and over, to anyone who would listen. Every morning, she'd ask me, "Where's my ring?"

One morning, finally deciding I had to do it, I left right after she asked me The Question. Going to the mall, I bought a $99 ring. When I got home, Gail was doing dishes.

I reached over the bar and handed it to her. "Here's your ring."

Her eyes lit up, and she snatched it out of my hand, immediately trying it on, admiring it from different angles. Then she called all her friends and family, announcing that she had a ring. I quietly left for work without her even noticing I was gone.

She was getting married because it was her dream. I was getting married because I had to.

Just after turning nineteen, my daughter was born. Red, wrinkly, and just the most beautiful thing in the world. I loved being a dad, and I loved being her dad. She was—and still is—perfect, and a turning point in my life. Another angel who saved me without ever knowing it.

When my daughter was one, and I'd just turned twenty, Gail and I split up. Life turned into a battlefield with her.

One night—I still don't know how—we ended up at a bar together. Cue too much to drink and we went home together, too. Two months later, she calls me.

She's pregnant again.

I'm absolutely positive I'm not the father. She's been dating, it's not like she's been hanging onto the memory of our time together.

I'd already decided to get a DNA test to make sure the baby's mine. When my uncle and I walk into that hospital room and see him for the first time, I knew—I definitely didn't need a test.

No DNA test was ever done. This kid looked like me. There's nobody in the world who looks more like me than this kid. Beyond that, I felt it. I had a son, and even as horrified as I was at that prospect of having to be a father to a son, something which I had no reference to from my own life, I was so proud to be this boy's father.

So, I had two kids with the same woman, and we were divorced when the second one arrived. Brother, I was not making things easy for myself.

I didn't know a thing about things like child support. Gail would call me up and tell me she needed diapers. Or she needed extra money to buy food. I'd be over with diapers or whatever cash I had. We lived near each other, so I'd see my kids all the time, and they stayed with me every other weekend. Sometimes more if Gail needed it, but that was the basic schedule.

Gail quit her job to go to school, went on welfare to help with that and the kids, and somewhere in there, a child support hearing was scheduled without me ever getting any notice.

I have to admit my responsibility for that. Because of how I grew up, and my main experience with work being modeling, I left my mom's house not even knowing how to sign a check. I don't know that I had ever seen a bill at that point, much less ever had to pay one. Things like paying legally required child support never even occurred to me.

Because I knew nothing about child support, I never suspected there would be something like a hearing about it. So, it's no surprise that I completely missed the hearing and nothing went in my favor. Of course, I didn't know how badly it had gone for me, because I never even knew it happened.

When my son was about a year old, I got a letter from the district attorney informing me that from now until my child support payments are up to date, they'll be garnishing my checks. They began by taking a quarter of my check, then upped it to half.

I was only bringing home $500 a month, and my rent was $250. When I told them I couldn't live on that, they gave me the lawyer equivalent of "Good luck."

I worked any and every job I could get my hands on, but without training, I could only get the shittiest paying jobs. At one point, I worked as a rock lifter. That means I lifted rocks with my body, so potential buyers could see the bottom to decide if they wanted it in their yard. Sometimes there were rattlesnakes under those rocks. Smashed fingers, spider bites, the occasional rattle snake... all for around minimum wage. Yes, that was an actual job in the late 80s, early 90s. Modeling it was not.

For part of this time, I found a bit of sanctuary under another angel's wing by the name of Beverly Eckert. Beverly was another girlfriend's mom, and she took the kids and I in, when my roommate suddenly moved out, leaving me with an apartment I couldn't afford. She loved me like her own son, even when her daughter and I split up. My son, Brandon, was a baby and pretty sick when I moved into Beverly's spare bedroom, and I don't know that I would have made it without her. Beverly spent many nights up with me, helping me take care of Brandon.

It was one of those times when you needed family and at that point my grandma had moved to Oklahoma to take care of her mom. My mom was out there as well, with her husband. I was again, pretty much on my own in figuring things out. Beverly did things like help me give the kids a Christmas one year when I was completely broke. She made sure they had a great Christmas and if not for her, they would have had none. She was always the first to lend a hand when I needed it. I did not know what I was doing as a father and she gave me the grace and time to figure it out. Like the other angels before her, my life would have ended up very differently without her in it.

I eventually ended up sharing a two-bedroom apartment with a friend, so when I had the kids, we'd all sleep together in my big bed. I'd pick them up and drop them at their mom's house and did the best I could to put food on the table.

Years later, when I had my own tiny apartment, I'd have times where rent was due at five pm on Friday. I'd slip a check into the box just at 5 to give myself the weekend to scratch together the money somehow. This didn't happen once. It happened several times, occasionally with different bills. I'd sometimes have to rush down to a utility office to pay a bill on time to ensure the service wasn't interrupted. I didn't always make it. Those were bad days.

Considering I wasn't eligible for food stamps or any sort of government assistance, life was more than tight for so many years.

Here's the thing about child support in California: Because of the interest and how they organize it, once you get behind, you can almost never catch up. There is also another little twist: If you get behind on your child support, they'll take your driver's license.

Exactly how that's supposed to help you catch up, I do not know. Without a car, how am I supposed to get to work? So, I did the only thing I could. I drove without a license for roughly nine years.

Never wanting to disappoint those ladies, I already lived a fairly straight and narrow life. Risking being caught driving without a license ensured I was the best driver I could be. My roommate also gave me his registration sticker every year. Back then, the police would usually only look at the color of the sticker on your license plate, not the actual number representing the year, so as long as you had the right color, you'd usually get by.

But if they catch you…

I was pulled over twice in those nine years. Both times, the officers had every right to take my car and take me to jail. In fact, it was their job to do those things. One of those officers was a man and one was a woman and in both instances, I just told them the truth. I was just trying to survive and not lose my kids. They both ran my name and had me sit in their car. It horrified me both times. But they both let me go. Both times I was given a good talking to, but

I also was given advice and in the case of the woman officer, I was given the number of an attorney that may be able to help me. But in both instances, I was allowed to drive away. I wasn't a bad guy. I was just struggling so hard.

Every single day, I was terrified Gail would find something out like that license thing and figure out some way to take my kids away. Every day was about dodging those kinds of bullets. Everything about those years was her trying to get revenge on me for... ruining her first marriage?

I'm not really sure what the grudge was. All I know is that it was there, it was real, and my ex-wife could get creative. Her family had money, and she married a pretty well-off man, so she had the funds to back her vengeful nature up.

Throughout this time, I will admit I really missed that Japanese 'fame' as my struggles grew and life went on. I missed what I thought I could have done with it. I'm sure the level of that fame grew in my imagination to be much larger than it really was, as life got harder, but I would fall back on times like that day at the train station or those trips on private planes, when things got really tough. Those times were real. In those moments at least, I felt important, like I was worth something. That is a rare feeling for a boy in the circumstance my life had given me, and it felt good. Now, feeling good was a rare feeling. It also made sense to me that money came with fame and if I had the fame again, I wouldn't be struggling and man, I was struggling.

Had I been a little more self aware, I would have realized that what I missed wasn't the fame–it was just being 'something.' For so long, through my early adult life, I felt like I lived up to the stereotype of nothingness that the little fatherless child from Corpus Christi, Texas, was always supposed to be. That's what I was always running from.

That feeling of nothingness. But in those days, I didn't have the ability or even the want to dredge my soul that deeply. I just wanted to feel like something again.

There were periods when it was hard to look my loved ones in the face. Even grandma. She repeatedly told me how proud of me she was. But I wasn't anything I felt like she could be proud of. I wasn't anything I felt like my kids or my friends or family could be proud of and worst of all; I wasn't proud of myself. Quite the contrary. I felt, in a very literal sense, like nothing. Just surviving and doing the best I could to be a good dad, but really just feeling worthless. This nothingness went on for years.

In those quiet moments at night, during the struggling years, when the kids were asleep and my thoughts would turn to all the 'what ifs,' I would promise myself that if I were ever again in a position of fame, I would use it for something good. I would do something with it.

I'd leave my mark on the world and I would make sure I would be the kind of 'something' that my grandmother could be proud of. As silly of a dream as that may sound for a grown man to have while his two kids slept in the one bedroom they all shared... that was the dream. At that point, that was about the biggest dream I thought I could ever dream.

Gail and I went in for mediation three times. The first time, it was over a pair of socks. She'd sent some new socks with my daughter, and when they went back, I put the wrong pair of socks in her bag. She took me to court in an effort to get full custody over socks.

It backfired.

The mediator thought an attempt at full custody over socks was so ridiculous, I got an extra day with the kids. Every other weekend, and Wednesdays.

I don't even remember why we went to mediation the second time. All I remember is that suddenly I had the kids every other Monday through Thursday and every other weekend.

The kids were shuttling between my little apartment and their mom's house during the school week, forcing them to take their clothes to school with them on pickup day. One day, as I picked them up, I asked a question.

"Can I bring them back on Fridays, just so they don't have to carry all their stuff at school?" I asked, hopeful that we could work together on a simple solution like this.

Gail lost her mind. She had recently moved into her 'dream home' and was now a good 45 minute drive from my house. Meaning a 90 minute round trip drive for me, with no driver's license. Her life had lined up to a point where she felt like she could finally take the kids from me, and if I'm honest, she was in the perfect position to do that. I was definitely on the ropes, so to speak. Later that week, I found out she'd paid a private mediator to take me back to mediation for a third and final time. It's my own opinion, but I think she thought she was essentially buying custody of the kids. Again, I was horrified.

The mediator investigated us for six weeks, interviewing and talking to people close to us. She spoke to each of the kids several times, which I'm sure was tough on them. The whole thing was tough to go through. In the end, she wrote a scathing review about my ex. And with that assessment by this well-respected mediator and psychologist, a tremendous weight lifted off me.

For the first time since our divorce, nearly fifteen years ago, someone in a position of authority finally saw what had been happening.

Because Gail would always talk to coaches, teachers, and other parents first, they'd all look at me like I was the most horrible person they knew. It was in their eyes, and you could feel it when I walked into a room to meet them for the first time.

By this point, any confidence I may have had in myself had been squashed out of me. In my mind, I was a failure on so many levels. If there is a level below nothing, that is what I felt like. So, to have a mediator Gail paid to investigate our situation, see me for who I really was, was... freeing. I got that report on the same day as a beauty pageant my daughter was in was taking place. There is a picture of us somewhere from that evening and although most wouldn't see it, there is such a pride and sense of relief in my smile in that photo. I hadn't smiled like that in years.

Then, we went to court one more time. Interestingly enough, each time we ended up in court, we had the same judge. I'm pretty sure he was tired of seeing us by this point. He read the mediator's report and announced that I'd receive full custody of my kids.

Her lawyer stood up, talking for several minutes about my motives, saying I only wanted custody for the money. While they were talking, I'm slowly crawling out of my skin, wanting nothing more than to jump up and shout, "I didn't even start this! I don't want any of that!"

My lawyer, sitting beside me, is calm, cool, and collected, thoroughly unfazed by her lawyer's ranting. He pats my leg under the table, whispering, "Shhhh... It's okay."

As soon as Gail's lawyer took their seat, the judged looked at me. "Mr. Hawley."

My lawyer rose, taking on the air of a courtroom drama, straightening his collar and tie, looking around the courtroom, nodding and smiling at everyone there, then he looked down at me, smiled and gave me a little wink, before looking back up at the judge.

In his calm, Southern drawl, he cleared his throat, straightened his tie one last time, lifted his head a bit and said, "Your Honor, Mr. Hawley declines any kind of financial support, thank you." and then he took his seat. That was it.

The judge immediately turned his full attention back to Gail and her side of the room, clearly not amused that he had to listen to fifteen minutes of pontification. This judge has seen me struggle to get every other weekend, to an extra day, to an extra four days. The mediator's report is still open in front of him.

You can clearly see him mentally tallying how much of his time she's wasted as he jots down a few notes. Then he looks over at me again. "Mr. Hawley, Are you sure you want to decline that?"

"I do."

"It comes out to roughly $1800 a month."

A huge sum at the time, particularly for a man who'd had to take extra work under the table just to make ends meet.

"I know, and I understand. I still decline. Thank you."

All I wanted was my kids and for this to all be over. And with that last statement, it was over.

After that day, things began to change. They canceled my child support back payments. I met another woman who gave me beautiful twin boys, and we moved to Oregon. I got my HVAC license. Not because I was thrilled about heating and air conditioning, but because when mine went out, I called a guy in, he worked for ten minutes; I paid him $400 and was happy to do it.

Yep, that was definitely a job for me.

In Oregon, I got a job at a resort in the little town of Silverton, where we had settled.

My then wife and I ended up going our separate ways, but this time, everything ended calmly and courteously, if not warmly. We are still friends to this day.

Then I met Mikee. She is the woman I'd always dreamed of meeting. I don't think we would have been ready for each other in our younger years, but we found each other at the perfect point of our lives, right when we were supposed to, and I am so grateful we did.

Now... I realize that was a long and winding road to get to this cat story, but you need to know who exactly it was that found this cat. Life had turned around by the time I found Sticky, but I had been through decades of feeling like a failure. Like nothing. I knew I was a good person, and I had some things to be proud of by this point, but I had also resigned myself to the fact that I would most likely do nothing of any consequence in this world.

I felt lucky to just make it out of my 20s and 30s. I was now a 48-year-old maintenance man with outstanding twin teenage boys, a beautiful wife and a couple of dogs. I was also still deep in the process of learning how to be proud of myself. I thought my 'consequential days' were long behind me and I was settling in to fade into the sunset. That's the guy that found this cat.

Now... on with the story.

2

OCTOBER 19, 2018

October 19, 2018

I sighed, pouring another cup of coffee to take to work with me. I had a meeting at 7:45 that I really didn't want to go to, but as director of facilities at The Salvation Army, even if I had nothing to contribute, I still had to be there.

My wife, Mikee, gave me a quick kiss. "Holla at your girl," she said.

I paused for half a second. Our usual goodbye was a simple "Holla". We still debate whether those extra few words were the magic that changed that day or not. I replied, "Holla at your boy," as I left the house.

The air had finally cooled, feeling truly like fall for the first time. A hot summer, followed by an Indian summer, meant the second thing I turned on when I got into the car was the heater.

As I drove down the two-lane farm road, that leads from my little town of Silverton, Oregon, to the big city of Salem, passing logging trucks, tractors, and large fields of grass seed that stretch out to the horizon on each side of the road, I searched my iTunes for something that would give me some kind of enthusiasm for the meeting.

Thumbing through Tom Petty, I remembered a conversation I'd just had with my boss the previous week. I'd made a Facebook post, expressing some frustration with my place in the world. Like, life was good, but it still didn't quite... fit. I didn't feel like I was fulfilling my 'purpose', although I wasn't sure what that was yet.

My boss had seen it and was really cool about it, more concerned with how I was feeling when he asked me, "If you could do anything in the world, what would it be?"

It was a question I'd already been thinking about, so I didn't hesitate. "I want to give people hope." How I'd give them hope, however, had me stumped. "Oprah's kind of got that job locked up," I joked. "And I don't know too many other people who could work 'hope' as a career."

I left his office feeling bad that he'd seen the post, but invigorated about posting it, anyway. I'd put the thought out into the Universe. That was really all I could do.

None of the songs I thumbed through were giving me the feeling I was looking for, something to carry me through a meeting, but at least it was Friday. As I got closer to Salem, the road I was on turned into four lanes, two each way. Just past the stoplight where it happened, I noticed cars driving over a little bit of something on the road.

I wrote it off as trash. After all, nobody was stopping or slowing, so what else could it be?

As I glanced back and forth between my stereo and the road, the white pickup truck just in front of me passed over that bit of trash. As it crossed over, the clouds opened slightly and sunlight hit my area. That piece of trash sat up, suddenly resolving into a kitten.

But it didn't look like a living kitten, more like the most stereotyped kitten outline you've ever seen. Except my mind didn't even have time to register it as a kitten. Instead, it went 'not trash!' and my foot automatically hit the brake.

It forced the cars behind me to slam on their brakes. Horns started blaring, but I barely heard them. My entire focus was on that little kitten on the road.

He'd lifted his head, and I kept going back and forth between "That's a kitten!" and "Where are my hazards?" I'd hit that hazard button by accident so many times, and now I couldn't find it. I fumbled all over my dash, hoping the little guy wouldn't try to run across the road, but it didn't budge.

I finally got my car in park and the hazards on. Meanwhile, the first car began moving around me as I flung my door open, intent on getting to that kitten before it tried to run across the road. "Stop! Stop, stop, stop!" I yelled, hoping the driver could hear me and wouldn't flatten that cat.

I can see the drivers looking at me, and "What the hell, man?", plainly written across their faces when I got out of my car.

"Hang on just a minute," I shouted, running around to the front of my car. The kitten is still sitting there and gave me the saddest little raspy meow I've ever heard. Poor guy looked wet, but when I picked him up, my hands got covered in some kind of goo. Weirdest of all, his back feet didn't move with the rest of him when I tried to scoop him up.

"Get out of the F*$#ing road!" a driver shouted at me as he passed.

"What do you think I'm doing? Picking up a quarter?" I yelled back, taking my focus off of the kitten for a minute.

That guy flipped me off, and other drivers were yelling, but honestly? What did they think was going on, seeing a man kneeling in front of a car? Obviously, everything isn't okay, otherwise I wouldn't be there. Nobody stopped to see if everything was all right, whether I needed help, nothing. It felt like I was on the road for hours, but in reality, it was probably only a few seconds.

I can finally see that he's completely covered in some kind of goo, with more on his back feet. He's stuck to the road. Now, I can see it's obviously glue, so much so that his paws looked like they had glue booties.

Well, now I knew why he hadn't tried running away.

Although this kitten was tiny. Maybe a month old, I figured he'd probably barely be walking, anyway. Pulling on his paws, I can see the little pads stretching, stuck to the road. It was easier to pull the glue booties from the road rather than remove the glue from him.

Getting what I thought was a 'her' at the time off of the road, I took him over to the side, assessing the situation. This little thing was shaking like a leaf, and I was afraid the cold would get him, but I still needed to get that glue off him. As I set him down, I tried to use the dewy grass to remove some of it, but the glue wouldn't budge. All I could see around was a run-down duplex.

No sign of other kittens, cats, or even people who might own or even take care of cats.

I scanned the area, then looked down at this tiny kitten sitting next to my foot, shivering. A giant orange and yellow leaf, still in perfect condition, just fallen from the tree, tumbled across the grass and blew smack right into him, completely wrapping around him, covering him in leaf.

You will not survive out here. No way you'll make it, I thought, shaking my head. At that moment, I knew this little guy was coming with me.

After getting the leaf off him, I put him in my shirt to warm him up and took him to work with me.

One lady I worked with, Elise, is a Super Cat Lady, and I desperately wanted to talk to her. Maybe she'd take this little guy. If not, she'd hopefully have some advice for this dedicated Dog Dad.

But even as I'm thinking that Elise might take the kitten, I can't get a conversation I'd had with Mikee about three days before. Our older dog, Jojo, had just come home from the vet. He had cancer, and we'd hoped the surgery would remove it.

It did not.

The cancer had spread too far, so we brought him home. Our only thought was to give him the best last few days we could. Lots of sleeping in his favorite spots, pets, and cuddling with this 110 pound Good Boy.

As I sat on the couch with my wife in the living room, we watched Jojo sleeping on his bed, Stewie, our Chihuahua, laying nearby. Stewie had been with and around Jojo for nearly his entire life. I didn't know what he'd do without the big old guy.

"Should we get another dog to keep Stewie company?" Mikee asked.

"Ya probably." I shook my head. "I think I want a cat though, too. Where should we go to get one?"

She tilted her head, watching the dogs. "I don't know. I think... I think cats kind of find you. Don't they?"

I thought about every cat I'd ever met. Independent, boss of their surroundings... and almost every one, a stray that had found me. "Yeah, I guess you're right. So, I guess if we're meant to have a cat, one will find me, huh?"

Now, driving to work with a kitten in my shirt, I couldn't help but think, A cat found me. A cat really found me. Can I actually give him away? Should I?

Putting aside whether I could, or should, give her the kitten, I went and found her, anyway. I needed her help to clean the little guy up, and he's so tiny, I don't even know what kind of food he can handle, or what's available.

I tracked her down in her office. I pulled him out of my shirt. She took one look and said, "I can't take another cat right now..."

Well. That answered that question. I have a cat now.

"Okay. But... how do we clean him up?"

We tried Goo Gone in the breakroom sink. I worked on his tail, but there's so much glue on him, I'd have to give him a bath in the stuff. I took a quick read of the directions, and I discover one really important instruction: Do not get on your skin.

Okay. We need to rethink how to clean him up.

Through it all, we talked about how he could have ended up on the road like that. With his small size, and how thoroughly he'd been stuck to the road, our best guess was that someone had done it to him. Covered him in glue and stuck him to a busy road in the early morning.

Man, someone was seriously screwed up.

Still unable to clean him off, Elise decided it was time she got back to work. "Maybe try your vet?" she suggested while cleaning her hands off.

"Yeah, that's a good idea. Thanks for your help!"

Silverton has two veterinary clinics. I called the one I thought was ours. Since we'd just had Jojo's surgery, our vet clinic knew us pretty well by now.

I didn't find out until later in the day I'd called the wrong vet, but they heard the story first.

"What?! You found a what?"

A kitten glued to the road.

Long pause. "Okay. Let me just check over our times today. I'll call you back shortly."

While waiting for them to call me back, the kitten climbed up onto my shoulder. He sat facing me, eyes closed, his head slowly tipping back, about ready to pass out. It looked like he was staring at me with pure gratitude, but in reality, he was falling asleep. He had been through a lot, and at the very least, had a really rough morning.

Unable to resist, I snapped a selfie and sent it to Mikee, telling her how I found him.

Holy crap! For real?

For real.

After a long pause, she typed back, We shall name him Sticky.

I laughed. Sticky. What a name, though it did suit him. Then, since I was waiting for the vet to call back, I did what we all do these days: posted about it on Facebook.

I had one hundred and twenty-eight friends, mostly local, and I figured a couple might share it, but I wanted to warn any of my friends heading into town about what had happened and to watch out. After all, if it was deliberately done (which seemed likely) then the person might have done it again.

I also partially called out all those people who'd zoomed past, just being jerks about everything. This wasn't nothing. I'd had a reason and a purpose in partially blocking traffic. Mostly, I just wanted people to relax and settle down.

Life has a habit of throwing some punches, and in the grand scheme of things, being two seconds late isn't really all that bad. Especially if it means helping something out.

That done, I decided I wasn't waiting for the vet to call me back. Sticky would not be able to rest and recuperate with all that glue stuck to him. Letting my guys know I'd be back later—and thankful I was the boss and able to leave if necessary—I headed to my car.

A buddy of mine texted before I left the parking lot.

Hey, man, can you make the post public? I want to share it.

After making it public, I texted, 'Done, brother. Thanks!'

Silverton only has those two vet clinics, and I headed straight to ours, on the outskirts of town. By this time, I had Sticky wrapped in a towel to keep the excess goo from getting all over my hands again, and took him straight to the receptionist.

"Hey," I said. "I called earlier about the glue covered kitten-"

"The what?!"

"... the cat... covered in glue. Didn't I talk to you guys earlier?"

Apparently, I had not.

After explaining the situation again, they took us into an examination room. They came to the same conclusion, too: someone had done this deliberately. They also found a thin slit around his neck, a tiny, perfect circle cut around.

We were discussing what could have caused it. I saw shock and horror on everyone's face, made even worse when one of the vet techs said, "It looks like this was caused by a fishing line."

Our best guess is that the person tied a fishing line around Sticky's neck and either swung or dragged him around.

And suddenly, we're all creeped out at the realization that someone absolutely did this to a five week old kitten, intentionally. How the hell does someone do that to a helpless creature?

I still hadn't shaken the feeling off when they took Sticky for a warm mineral oil bath to take the glue off and left me alone in the examination room.

I'd barely sat down when messages began coming in. Local friends, mostly, asking for updates on the kitten. My post had just over two hundred likes, and it'd been barely an hour. My most liked post before that had been my wedding, which, between Mikee and I, got about two hundred and fifty.

I answered questions, responded to comments, and tried to figure out if someone else had found a kitten, too? Maybe that was why it had gotten so popular?

A vet tech walked into the room, smiling. "You've got a phone call. Channel 12 News wants to talk to you."

"About what?"

"About the kitten."

"How do they know about that?" I stared up at her, confused. How could Channel 12 News know about Sticky? Why would they want to talk to me about him?

"They saw your Facebook post," she said.

"... How did they know I was here?"

"They didn't. The reporter said they've been calling every vet around. It's just luck you were here when they called."

This day just kept getting stranger and stranger.

"You could talk to them," I suggested, my phone buzzing in my hand again.

She left the room, but she came back a minute later. "They really want to talk to you," she said, handing me a piece of paper.

It had the reporter's name and number, and a message saying she wanted to meet up with me where I'd found Sticky. So, I called her back and set up a time for later that afternoon, on my way back to work.

It wasn't long before the vet had the last of the glue off Sticky, and I went to the interview with my new buddy. It took barely five minutes, just chatting on the side of the road with a camera pointed at me. Right after that interview, we called the police, because by this time, we were sure that Sticky had been left intentionally, and we noticed a traffic camera on the light not too far away.

That evening, on my way home, I stopped one more time near the intersection of Silverton Road and Cordon, this time to meet the police. I showed them where I saw Sticky and where I'd stopped.

A small stand of trees stood about fifty feet away, and they pointed to it. "Did you notice someone standing over there?"

"Dude, I just found a cat covered in glue. You could've been here in a clown suit, and I wouldn't have seen you." Between the cat, the cars, the drivers yelling, and trying to figure out what, exactly, I was looking at, I had had little space to notice other things.

"The person who did it was probably standing there, watching," the officer said. "People like that want to see the results of their...work."

"Seriously?"

"Sadly, yes."

And the creepiness factor just rose to a whole new level.

Then they checked out the traffic camera and determined that you'd have to be standing far out in traffic to be seen by it. This guy put Sticky too close to the side of the road to pick him up.

So, I shook their hands, thanked them, and took my little buddy home to meet his new family.

It turned out Sticky fit right in. This poor, traumatized kitten took one look at the biggest animal in the house, Jojo, a one hundred and ten pound Great Pyrenees, and curled up against his belly. At first, we were afraid that Jojo was just too doped up after his surgery to respond normally, but he seemed to look at this tiny, five week old kitten and think, "Just be still."

Occasionally, over the next few days, you'd hear a loud WOOF! We'd come running to find Sticky attempting to nurse on our elderly cancer patient. Jojo just looked up at us as if to say, "For real?"

As crazy as the day was, it came so close to never happening. It all happened because once, a kindly old lady thought I was Roger.

3

BEING ROGER

B eing Roger

The circumstances that ensured I'd be on Silverton Road on that Friday morning can be traced back to a single day roughly four years before.

I was looking for a new job after getting back from Hawaii, visiting my grandma in a care home where she had finally settled to live out her last days. I only had a couple of weeks to find a new position, but I still wanted something that would let me help people.

Part of it was just seeing Grandma. Her care home was pleasant, and the staff there were friendly and kind to her, but I hated her being so far away, where I couldn't go over every day, or even every weekend, to help her. I hated thinking about how lonely she must get some days.

So, as I was job hunting, while I had a few interviews lined up, I was really interested in the last one, as maintenance manager at a memory care home in the town of Woodburn, Oregon. I felt that if I couldn't help Grandma, then maybe I could help someone else in her position. At the very least, I could make sure they were comfortable and everything around them stayed in good working condition.

After talking to the facility's manager, I was confident I had the job, but I still needed to go in for that interview.

I arrived early, just to take the time to check out the property. As I walked around, I saw several residents being taken for walks. Some of them were obviously with staff, while others were with who I thought could be family.

Benches sat out on the perfectly trimmed park-like setting they had, as the gardeners trimmed and pruned their way around the property. There was a lot of activity, although it somehow all seemed very slow.

Two glass double doors led into the main building, where I waited while I the receptionist buzzed me in. I appreciated the fact that they kept it secure.

When I approached the receptionist's desk, she barely looked up.

"Hi," I said. "I'm Chuck Hawley. I know I'm early. I'm here to see Mr. Jones."

To the right of the desk, I can see an open door leading to an office. A man at a desk was barely visible, but since I'd never seen Mr. Jones, I didn't know if this was him or not.

"Yeah, sure," the receptionist said. "You can wait there." She waved vaguely, somehow indicating the entire area and nowhere all at once.

I glanced around at the main lobby. A small, blue and white couch sat against the far wall, covered in a pile of clean laundry. At the far end, past some potted plants, the lobby changed to look like a living area. I could see a long couch on the far side with a woman sitting at one end. There were no other available seats, so I headed for that couch.

After a quick look back at the receptionist, who still hadn't looked up, I headed into the room. I found an elderly lady sitting on the other end of the couch. She stared out the window with a vacant expression. It was the same vacant stare I'd seen on many of the residents in the yard. I sat, figuring I wouldn't disturb her—she didn't seem likely to even notice me—waiting for my interview and surveying the room.

I can't say the place only had seventies vibes, but it was more like they'd picked up a seventies living room and transplanted it to 2014. There was no way this décor had happened by accident. Stepping from the lobby into the living room was like entering a time capsule.

The couch had that dark floral print that was popular in the seventies and eighties. There were large oil paintings with landscape scenes, and the flooring somehow... matched. Only the giant, flat-screen TV on the wall let you know you hadn't traveled back in time.

As I thought about the average age of the residents I'd seen, I figured they must have deliberately done this to prevent confusion for the residents. It all reminded me of my childhood and suddenly, I missed Grandma very much. I looked over at the lady, hoping she had people who came to visit her, who reminded her of better times and would make sure she wasn't lonely.

Without meaning to, I began making plans to visit this lady when I got this job. It could be a way of visiting Grandma, and if I could make sure this lady wasn't lonely, maybe Grandma somehow wouldn't be, either.

The woman I'd been watching turned and saw me. She smiled reflexively, and I smiled back. Her eyes, so vacant, suddenly filled with life. It was as if her soul woke up.

"Roger!" she exclaimed, looking at me as if I were her long-lost friend.

I smiled. Normally, I'd probably try to gently correct her and get out of there, but this time, "Hi there." popped out of my mouth.

"Oh! Where have you been?" She began talking about people she and Roger knew, and I struggled to play along.

She seemed so happy to see Roger and I didn't want to disappoint her, but I also didn't know if I could pull off this acting job I'd just committed myself to. What should I do now? I was going to be Roger for a few minutes.

Playing along like this was very out of character for me, but this sweet old lady reminded me so much of Grandma, and I had nothing else to do for a few minutes. She looked so happy to see 'Roger'.

I would not be the one to take that beautiful smile from her.

"Cindy went to the church's bake sale with Barbara last week, and Barbara's brownies sold right out!"

At first, I couldn't pay much attention to what the woman said. I was too busy watching her for cues, laughing with her, thinking this wouldn't last long. After all, I had my interview soon with Mr. Jones, and how long could this lonely woman last before the light went out of her eyes again?

But the more she spoke, the more she sank into these memories, seeing them as if they were happening right now. As I looked

around the room, I realized she probably told these stories every day to anyone who would sit and listen.

Soon, it sounded more like a Hallmark movie, a quaint little town, very Norman Rockwell-esque stories, and I relaxed into the flow of things. I got comfortable enough to throw in an "Oh, my gosh!" or a "Sure," here and there as she talked about a life that she must miss very much. I really enjoyed talking with her. It was like we really were in some kind of holiday movie, just making up characters and quaint little scenes.

As she spoke, a little thought started up at the back of my mind. I was already growing attached to this woman, with her beautiful smile and her wonderful, calming stories. How much more attached would I get if I worked here?

Then, I heard my name called. Leaning out to see around a potted plant, I saw Mr. Jones standing in the small lobby, glancing around. I checked my phone, but I still had a few minutes until the start of the interview, so I waved but didn't get up.

Mr. Jones never noticed me and went back into his office, and I went back to thinking about what having this job would be like. I could visit this sweet old lady nearly every day. I could hear these stories told to Roger again and again. Maybe I would be a different person to her every time I saw her. I didn't know who she was talking about, but she certainly did.

Had you just watched this woman from across the room, you would have seen an empty shell of an old lady, staring blankly out the window. No one could blame you for thinking she had always been in this care home. That she had no life to remember before spending her days sitting in a kind of movie set meant to remind her and her forced roommates of a time long gone.

But of course she did.

She was a wife, mother, friend, sister, daughter... She volunteered at her church and played piano. She had a dog – many dogs, that she shared her life with. These things were gone now. Her life consisted of this simulated world, made to look like her past life, but without the hope that tomorrow might be a better day. It wouldn't get any better than today or yesterday... the days would always be the same. That is, unless she ran into a long-lost friend to talk with for a while. Today, that friend was Roger.

As I listened to her and pretended to be Roger, I realized that this sad existence was what I would come to every day. Sure, I could help her by making sure her room was in good shape and I could listen to her from time to time and pretend to be Roger, but I couldn't fix this for her. And it would fix nothing for my grandmother. I couldn't change any of these folks' circumstances for them.

And then I'd have to watch her pass away, because that's why she was here. Every resident was there because their condition was so bad, or they're so old that they were at the end stages of life. They're there to die.

This job could crush me.

To care for these residents, see my grandma somewhere in each of them, and then watch them all pass away, one at a time? Then greet new ones, knowing they'd die soon, too? I began trying to figure out ways to get myself out of a job that was a sure thing.

Except I really needed a job. Saying No would be irresponsible.

Mr. Jones came out of his office again, calling my name. I half-waved at him and looked right at the receptionist. She's staring past Mr. Jones, right at me, but never pointed me out to him, or did anything to show him where I was.

I waved a little again, but Mr. Jones just returned to his office. I felt relieved. No way I could get the job if I missed the interview, right? Because I didn't want this job anymore.

"Well," I gently stopped her before she could go into another story, "I should get back to work soon."

"Oh." She regarded me for a moment. "How is work?"

"Work is great. They're keeping me busy." I said, smiling at her.

"And your car? I know you love your car. So bold. Race car red." She gave a little laugh.

"Oh, yes... still have the car."

Still grinning, she reminisced over Roger's car—race car red was the only description she had. She laughed, so I laughed again and nodded along as I settled back in to listen to her talk about a stretch of road I had never heard of or driven down. It didn't matter. At this point I was listening to this woman's stories, just hoping somehow that my grandmother, three thousand miles away, maybe wouldn't feel quite as alone. I hope it worked.

I stumbled through answering questions, sifting through what she said, trying to figure out what kind of car it was, but I couldn't really come up with a make or model. Just that I loved that car and it was race car red.

Finally, I said, "Well, I gotta get back to work. It was really good to see you."

The change that happened next shook me a little. She shut down, like a robot when you hit the power button. She went from lively, interested, and talking, to staring at the floor.

When I got up, I took her hand and held it a minute. "It was really good seeing you again. I hope I see you again tomorrow."

"Yes, I hope so," she said, but it wasn't the same as she'd been earlier, when she was living in the past. She seemed very tired as she said, "we will talk more tomorrow, Roger."

I squeezed her hand, smiled at her and said, "Yeah, we will."

"Bless your heart," she murmured as I walked away. One of my grandmother's favorite sayings.

When I turned back for one last look, she'd gone back to staring out the window. Everything that made her, her... asleep again.

I felt so drained as I headed towards the doors, figuring I'd try to sneak out since my interview should have started at least fifteen minutes ago. As I walked past the receptionist, she looked up.

"Mr. Jones missed you," she said.

I glanced back at the office door and I could see he'd looked up, so I stuck my head in. "Hey, sorry I'm late. I was sitting in your living area, talking to one of your residents."

He gave me a vaguely annoyed look, as if he were trying to figure out who I was talking to.

"So, anyway," I continued, "I am still available for that interview. But I probably don't have this gig. I get it. That's okay."

"I can't do the interview now," he said. "I have another one in..." he checked his watch, "... ten minutes."

"That's okay. Call me if you want me to set up another one, but if not, I understand."

"No." He shuffled papers on his desk. "Let's set one up now. Are you available this Wednesday?"

Two days. Ugh. This wasn't a job I wanted anymore, but I needed one. I'd already left my last job. I had nothing else lined up, so...

"Sure, no problem. Same time?"

"Same time," he confirmed.

But the entire drive home, I kept replaying what it was like, sitting with that woman. It was so out of character for me to have played along, or even to have sat next to her.

It was one of those things that felt like it was supposed to happen. I just... I had to find another job. I couldn't do that one.

As soon as I got home, I logged onto Craigslist. The very first one I saw was for maintenance at the Salem Salvation Army community center. I called the number and talked my way into an interview that afternoon. By the next day, Tuesday, I had the job.

The best part was that I could still help people, but in a way that worked better for me. It wouldn't be so emotionally draining and I wouldn't be seeing my grandma in every person who came through the place.

I called Mr. Jones back and told him my good news. He got mad.

"Sorry, brother," I said. "I don't know what to tell you."

"Do you at least know anybody else who's looking for a job like this?"

"No, I don't. Sorry."

After hanging up with him, I had the feeling I'd really dodged a bullet there, not just with the residents, but dealing with him.

And I could only think that it was all because of talking with the woman for those fifteen to twenty minutes. If I'd arrived and just gone straight to see Mr. Jones, I might've been there for years before I finally left, burnt-out, and exhausted.

If I had interrupted that very sweet woman who thought she was getting the chance to visit with someone from her past, I would have most likely gotten that job at the care home and not looked for another option, or at least missed that chance to work at the Salvation Army.

If I had never worked at the Salvation Army, I would have been driving a different direction than I was on the morning that I found Sticky, which means I would have never found him. And if I had never found Sticky, none of the things his story is responsible for would have ever happened.

I firmly believe all of those things that happened the day that I pretended to be Roger for a few minutes happened so all the things that have happened since could come to life. Being Roger is the moment this story really started.

4

FAMOUS AGAIN...

Famous again...

    I didn't look at Facebook very often in those days. A couple of times a month. It was never important, and I never got much interaction. I just liked to see what my friends were up to.

The day after I found Sticky, we went to my father-in-law's house to help him around the yard for the day. Around mid-morning, my wife comes out, holding her phone.

"Hey, did you look at your post lately?"

I shrugged. Not since the day before.

"You've got eighteen thousand likes."

I stared at her. "What do you mean?" I only had a hundred and twenty-eight friends. "How could I possibly get that many likes on it?"

"I don't know," she said, shaking her head, "but it does."

When we broke for lunch, I checked out the post. "Uh, honey," I said, scrolling through, "I thought you said I had eighteen thousand likes."

"Yeah." She said.

"It's up to thirty-five thousand," as I showed her the post.

While it was weird, it certainly wasn't something, yet. Finding a kitten hadn't become an event. I'd simply picked up a kitten when it needed it, just like millions of people do every year.

That night, a second news story was on a different news station, and texts began rolling in from farther away friends. Just little things.

I saw you on the news!

Good job.

How's the kitten?

Things like that.

It shocked me when a friend from Virginia messaged. "Where are you seeing this?" I asked. "How do you even know about it?"

"It's on the internet," they replied.

By Sunday night, somewhere around a hundred thousand people had liked and commented on that post from Friday. It was becoming an event. On Monday, I had a single message request from England.

England. I didn't know anyone there.

And then my message requests exploded. I couldn't keep up with them, but that almost didn't matter because they had a common theme: You're a hero.

That was the craziest thing to me and really very uncomfortable. I didn't think I was a hero. I picked a cat up. Over the years, I have probably rescued twenty cats. I know people who have rescued hundreds. None of them ever ended up in the news or with this level of notoriety, much less thought of as a hero.

I spent so much time trying to understand why people were so fascinated by this one story. I hadn't rushed into a burning building to save this kitten. I just stopped on a moderately busy road, grabbed a kitten and then posted a photo that I'd taken for my wife.

That Monday morning, it started dawning on me, however, that for whatever reason, this really touched people's hearts, but the size of it all didn't sink in until the afternoon.

Around mid-afternoon, my phone rang. When I looked at it, I saw a weird number, but I answered it anyway. A guy with a thick Australian accent starts talking.

"Hey, mate, it's Jimbo with SBS Radio 1Australia! How you doin'?"

"... good." Australia?!

"Hey, you're the cat guy, right?"

I pulled the phone away from my ear, staring at it. Cat guy? Who do you think I am? Then again, if he meant, guy who found a cat, then... "Yeah. So... where are you?"

"Australia, mate!"

"How did you get my number?"

Jimbo laughed. "I got it off Facebook. You probably want to hide that, mate."

Oh, no! When had I... My buddy had asked me to make the post public. Had that made my entire profile public, too?

"I can see everything about you on there, mate. Not a good way to have your profile when you're going viral." I was going viral? I can hear the humor in Jimbo's voice. I don't really understand how Facebook works but out of everyone who's been messaging me, he's the first person to tell me they can see all my information. That alone showed me he was a real person, and a pretty decent one.

After a minute of talking about my profile, he got to the reason for the call. "Yeah, mate, so we heard about you and the kitten. I just wanted to get your story, mate. Over here, people can't get enough, y'know?"

I ran through the story for him, but when I got to the part where Elise and I were trying to use the Goo Gone on Sticky, the call suddenly dropped. While I waited to see if he'd call me back, I ran to Facebook, and sure enough, my information was all visible.

Suddenly, I had to figure out how to make my information private, and I'd barely done that when Jimbo called back. We spoke for another minute, then a static click, then the call dropped again. There was no third callback.

I stared at my phone. Holy crap! I just got called by a radio station in Australia!

This was my first hint at how far this had really spread, but in my mind... I was just a guy who had found a cat.

That night, I got a bunch of phone calls and messages from various other news outlets. During that first week, I gave thirty-five to forty interviews, lots of them to radio stations.

One was in Santa Cruz, California, and they played a game with me and their listeners. The listeners had to guess who I was based on clues given, one at a time. They even had a $500 cash prize on it.

I laughed. "Man, you should've offered a million. There's no way anyone is going to guess it's me!"

But they only got to their second clue when the caller said, "It's that guy that just found the cat in Oregon!"

Wow. What has happened to my life?

While most of the interviews that first week were over the phone and on radio stations, I had a few local news reporters that came to my house. One of them really stood out.

I sat in my living room with the reporter while things were being set up, and first off, I had to shake my head. Already, strangers setting filming equipment up in my living room had become a thing that people just did in our home.

I sat, chatting with the reporter while his camera guy set up around us, and I said, "You know, I still don't get why this story is so popular. Like, I don't understand how it has gone this far."

He didn't look up from a monitor type device. "You know you were on the Iraqi news last night, right?"

"No..."

"It's true."

"What?" I shook my head. "You're telling me they didn't have anything bigger going on over there than a dude and his cat?"

He looked right at me. "You're giving people hope," he said.

I immediately got chills. It'd been about two weeks since I had sat in my boss's office and said I wanted to give people hope. All I wanted to do was give people hope, and then, what he said...

He gave me a little smile. "Who needs hope more than those people over there?"

That changed everything for me. Until this point, all the interest and news coverage we were getting was the silliest thing in the world. The realization that I'm now giving hope to people in a war-ravaged country is... It's huge.

I switched from, "Yeah, okay, I'll humor you," to, "Let's do this. Let's see what we can create with this one simple story." It also changed how I felt about the interview itself. Until then, I always felt goofy, like everything was just blown all out of proportion. For the first time, I had a purpose here, and a message to share.

Goodness out of Spite

While I was running around giving a bunch of interviews without really understanding why all these people were interested, my wife's friend, Lori, decided to help out, too.

Jojo's surgery cost us around $3000, and now we had a new kitten with some issues of his own, like being mostly deaf. Lori set up a GoFundMe to help us recoup some of what we'd spent on Jojo, or use it for anything Sticky might need.

She made the GoFundMe, posted it online, and the responses were immediate. Lots of people wanted to help, and if this was how they could do it, then they did. So many people were so supportive. But there were others.

We got a few comments that were variations on, "Oh, now the truth is out! Watch them try to make money off this whole thing." It was as if they thought me finding Sticky was a stunt or something we had planned. I could have never even thought of this, much less planned it out and made it go viral, but there were a few folks that were sure I made this up.

There was even a pretty well known conspiracy type podcast host that had tried to prove this was all made up. He gave me the nickname, 'Cheeseburger Chuck'. The only thing that was true on his entire show about me was that I did, in fact, like cheeseburgers.

Mikee is an enigma. She is as tough as they come, and can be a hard one to win over. She can be quite intimidating to people when they first meet her, and it's nothing she does on purpose. It's just who she is.

But she has an enormous heart and will do just about anything for anyone that may need some help. She is a fierce defender of the people she cares about, and once she has been 'sent for', there isn't much stopping her.

The smack talking didn't sit well with her, and she decided we would not touch a cent for our own bills. Instead, she took all the money the site had raised and turned it into a charitable foundation, the Sticky the Kitty Foundation.

Its aim is to help low-income families afford a pet. The Foundation assists them with pet care, emergency vet bills, and whatever else they need so that these families can keep their pets healthy while teaching the children of these families what it is to take care of something, love, and be loved.

I loved the fact that something so good came from Mikee being so pissed off. It's really a case of goodness out of spite.

As of the writing of this book, the Sticky the Kitty Foundation is still going strong. The Foundation recently transitioned from individual help to helping organizations that are helping animals like rescues and sanctuaries or–'helping those who help the helpless' - as I like to say.

Mikee and her big heart have helped hundreds of people in the last few years, and been responsible for some amazing 'anonymous donations' that have made some enormous differences. She's been a savior to many who have never known it, and I couldn't be more proud of that beautiful, spiteful angel.

The Guy that Lived

One week after I found Sticky, we went to Sacramento to visit the family. Near the end of the weekend, I scrolled through the thousands of message requests I'd gotten through Facebook. I'd developed a set of criteria for responding to those, although I played it loose with that. The profiles had to have a picture, and then I'd glance at the first few words to see what they said.

If it started with "You're a hero," I usually scrolled past. I didn't feel like a hero. Also, if it didn't have a profile picture, I usually scrolled past it. Those didn't seem to be real to me. I had so many requests, though, there was no way I could ever keep up with them all. At some point, that criteria got thrown out the window, and which ones got opened all became kind of random.

Something about this one message that didn't have a profile picture caught my eye. I could only see the first few words - "I have found humanity in you". I had not seen those words in any of these messages yet. So I clicked on it. It was from a man in the UK who said he'd been preparing to commit suicide when he'd looked up and had seen my picture on the news.

This man wrote of how he stopped what he was doing long enough to see why this kitten was sitting on my shoulder in that photo. He told me how reading the story of Sticky and I had renewed a bit of his faith in humanity and given him hope. As I read through his message, I came to, "you will never know what this story has done for me but I stopped. You have saved my life."

I was stunned. Just completely shocked by the enormity of this message. Reading that was one of the most profound moments of my life. It was a life changer. It was the moment I realized I had always been someone. I can't tell you why it took something that huge for me to suddenly believe I had worth to this planet, but it was that message that made me believe that.

If I, just being me and helping a little kitten, was enough to stop someone from committing suicide, and I was still the same me I'd always been, then I'd always been someone worth something. I'd always had this ability to bring meaning into people's lives and to give hope. Even at my most 'nothingness', when I had felt the most useless, I had always been someone. I just never let myself believe it.

I also realized in that moment that we ALL must have this capacity to be great and amazing in small ways. We could all change someone's life for the better, no matter who you were, and it was as simple as being kind. It was like some mystical book of knowledge had opened up in front of me. Kindness was the answer. To everything. Not every act of kindness will reach the levels of notoriety that this one did and honestly, I still don't know that what I did is supposed to—but that doesn't mean we waste all of those acts of kindness.

Smiling at a someone, waving first, holding the door for a person who needs it and moving on, these things all pile up and create a kind of butterfly effect on the world. A kind of ripple that starts with that act of kindness being 'thrown into the pond.'

This time that ripple had traveled from a road in Oregon, all the way to the computer screen of a man in the UK that just needed some hope in that moment. And I had tossed that stone into the pond without ever even knowing it.

Reading the man's message of hope for his future hit me so hard, I started crying. My uncle came around the corner and caught me.

"Chucky boy." He came up to me. "What's wrong?"

I tried reading the message to him and couldn't, so I handed him my phone.

He read it. "Oh, man, Chucky. That's huge." He gave me the biggest hug. Then he pulled back. "Okay, dude. You gotta knock this crying thing off, though. Come on, Chucky, pull it together, man." He laughed a little, patting my back.

By now you have realized, and I will admit, there was a lot of crying involved in all of this. I was just overwhelmed with emotion for weeks. So much goodness coming at me, 24 hours a day. So much that you couldn't keep up with it all. I had never experienced anything like that. It was overwhelming, to say the least.

When I finally calmed down, I messaged this guy back. 'Please, don't give up... I'm learning as we go through this that there's a lot of shitty people in the world, but for every horrible person who would do this to this cat, there's a million people that would have stopped it. I have proof of it right here on this post. Here's three hundred thousand people that would have stopped too, so please don't give up.'

We messaged on and off for the next few weeks, but slowly, we lost touch. I couldn't always find his messages under the avalanche that continued to flood Messenger.

In the last messages I saw from him, he was very upbeat and full of hope. I don't know where he is now, but I know he had as profound an effect on me as I did on him, and I like to think we were in each other's lives at the exact moment and time we needed to be.

Talking to him really drove home the opportunity and responsibility I suddenly had. It went from a crazy story that I'll roll with for as long as it's bringing some joy and hope to people, into deciding that I'd actively do things with my story and this newfound 'fame'.

I started rolling ideas around, deciding who and how I could help the most, and although not fully formed or thought out, a lot of ideas began to appear.

The Cat Guy

Over the days and months after finding Sticky, I slowly morphed into the Cat Guy, as I was first called by that Aussie radio disc jockey. It happened everywhere and started the week after I found him.

Going to Sacramento that first week after finding Sticky, we were stuck in Friday afternoon rush hour traffic. It had been a fun drive down with my boys reading comments from that post, which had gotten to over a hundred thousand by this point.

We talked a lot about how our actions and even intentions travel on far past their intended target. Both good and bad actions create a kind of butterfly effect on everyone around you. Here, we were seeing just how far kindness could spread and how easy it was to make that kind of difference.

Because this person was kind to you, you smiled at the next person you met, brightening their day. Then, that person buys coffee for the next person in line in the drive through, that person then helps someone buy their groceries, and it continues on down the line.

Because of this instant, internet fame thing we had going, we had a much better view of how far it all spread, with people commenting about how they'd made a donation to a local cat shelter in Sticky's name, or checked in to see if an older person needed help, or even spoke more kindly to everyone they met in their day.

People all over the planet were suddenly being kind to each other. Because someone had shown a little kindness to a little kitten on a road in Oregon. It was really cool to show my kids firsthand how that worked, and it felt good to be the central part of that story.

Arriving in Sacramento and sitting in that Friday afternoon traffic, a convertible pulled forward on our left with two kids in the backseat. We caught each other looking at one another, and their eyes suddenly grew as they slowly looked back and forth between their phones and me.

It had been a week since I had found Sticky and I had grown used to the grocery store conversations and random recognition in my little part of the world, but we were sitting at a stoplight in a different state. One of my boys noticed their reaction and said, "They have seen the cat guy..." as we all laughed. I wasn't sure if that was it, but it sure seemed like it.

As the red light turned green, they slowly pulled ahead of us, now looking at our Oregon license plate on the front of our car. One of them began excitedly tapping the shoulders of the grownups in the front seat and as we passed, this carload of people began smiling and waving at us like I was their best friend. They honked as one boy showed me his phone and, sure enough, there Sticky and I were on his screen. They had indeed seen the cat guy.

And just like that, I knew what grandma had always been saying. I knew what to do with this fame, and it was so much cooler than the first time. Like I had a new superpower. I could make a kid's day just by smiling and waving. That family's trip just went from 'normal, stuck in traffic' to "we saw the cat guy!"

It was the first time I'd felt like that 'someone' I had been missing in 30 something years. But it was different this time. As embarrassing as it is to admit, when I had signed those autographs or got recognized during my time modeling, I really felt like I was more special than everyone around me.

That's not what I felt like now at all. It was humbling. I felt lucky. It felt like the universe had given me some kind of gift that made everyone smile, and I was grateful to share it. I knew what to do with the 'fame' this time.

From then on, people recognized me everywhere I went, at least for the next few months. In the grocery store, parking lots, on airplanes, restaurants, you name it, if I was there, someone recognized me.

People wanted to send Sticky gifts, so we had to rent a mailbox at a local mail house. One day as I picked up the mail, the guy that ran it said, "I'll give you $1000 for that cat." "Nah" I said. "He's not for sale."

"You wouldn't take $1000 for that cat?" he asked, like I was insane.

"Why would you offer $1000 for this cat?" I asked, thinking he was equally insane.

"Because I need a mouser," he replied. $1000 for a thrown away cat. I declined the offer and still wouldn't sell him. For any amount.

Once, Mikee and I were out grocery shopping. We'd just climbed into the car and we're talking about our next stop when someone drummed on the window. I looked over to see a woman practically pressing her nose against the glass, a huge grin on her face.

"Hi Chuck!" she called.

I rolled down my window. "Hi how are you?."

She had a gift card she had been carrying around, hoping she would run into me in our small town. We thanked her for the gift and chatted for a minute and then she moved on, grinning. Moments like that became common, and Mikee just learned to roll with it all. You couldn't have a better partner to experience sudden cat fame with.

Another time, I had gone to Nevada with my daughter to help my mom move from Las Vegas to Oregon. The trip proved uneventful, and we stopped in Bakersfield at a McDonald's grabbing an early breakfast. We'd left Vegas really early in our Uhaul truck, and we were hungry by the time we stopped at six thirty.

The parking lot was already pretty full with the cars of travelers and a few tour buses. We walked inside and got in one of the long lines. After a minute or so, I noticed someone doing the now classic double-take, and it spread from there. There were stares and people whispering behind their hands, watching us the whole time.

But no one said anything to us.

Back outside, I looked at my daughter, both of us laughing. Random strangers coming up to me had almost become normal, but I hadn't experienced the whispering and stares. It was weird.

As we walked to our truck, a couple who had been staring at me was walking ahead of us. The wife turned around. "Do you go to the boat show in Vegas?"

"Nope. Never been to that one."

The man turned around, smiling and sure he had figured it out. "Do you hang out with Steve and Brian from the shop?"

"No, I don't think so. I'm from Oregon." I said, as my daughter and I climbed into our truck, the couple standing by their own car.

Their smiles grew. Pointing, the wife said, "Oh you're that guy..." as I waved and shut the truck door. We backed out, leaving the couple smiling and their morning a little brighter, because of a chance encounter with the 'cat guy', in a dusty McDonald's parking lot in Bakersfield, California. Keep your eyes open, friends... you never know who you might come across on any day.

The emails and messages never seemed to stop. People needed a quick message of hope, or a bit of advice. Sometimes, I think they just needed to be heard.

One that stands out came from a guy in Scotland. It was a brief email, beginning with "Mr. Hawley," and he talked about how this story had somehow reunited him with his father after ten years of not speaking to each other. Telling me I wouldn't understand all the reasons, he explained he had gone to see his father after reading my story, only to find out his dad had cancer.

He didn't know how much time he had left, but because of the Sticky story, he would spend the rest of his father's days making up for lost time. He finished with "cancer's a (insert your favorite Scottish expletive here), Cheers."... an ode not only to his father but to Jojo as well, and then signed his name. So perfectly Scottish.

His wasn't the only random message that contained some pretty personal information. I found myself doing a bit of amateur counseling, too, but I'm giving it my best because... they asked for help. What else can I do?

You would be amazed at the amount of people that just need to hear the words, "You're going to be okay" even when it's said by a stranger. I heard from kids angry with their parents, parents angry with their kids... parents worried about their kids. I don't know why, but people suddenly felt like I had the answers to all of their problems.

A young woman wanted to come out to her family, but the thought that her family might disown her horrified her. We talked for several days, and on my side, I can't even remember what I said because it was nothing special or profound to anyone but her. I'm sure I encouraged her to always be herself. That's what I would encourage anyone to do.

She came out, and everything turned out cool, but it blew my mind that she wanted to talk to me about such a personal decision. That she trusted me to help her with that. I've never had to come out like that, so my experience doing it is exactly zero. I'm just glad I could help.

I had many folks contact me about how to deal with various bullying incidents. People felt like I maybe had the answers to dealing with bullies because I had stood up for Sticky. My standard advice, stand up to them. Always. If nothing else, you'll learn there is only so much they can do. Of course, be kind. But when that doesn't work, stand up to them.

I helped a man from the mid-west understand his 'liberal' son. Really, all I was helping him understand was that his son wanted peace and love in the world. Dad wasn't wrong about wanting the conservative ideals he wanted to live by. But his son wasn't wrong either. And why did it matter? In the end, it was his son, and he loved him. What else matters?

This is a good point to remind you, this whole story is happening to a guy who for 30 years of his life thought the biggest difference he could make in the world, was to make sure he didn't disappoint a few folks who cared about him. None of this was ever even remotely on his radar, and if you had told him all of this was coming, he would have thought you were nuts. Ok, back to the story...

People came to me with just about every manner of problem or issue you can think of, but a lot of times it was just for money. So many people asked for money. Not from the foundation. From me. I don't know why, but so many people thought we suddenly had money. Like Sticky came with a treasure chest attached to him. He came with a horribly sad story and a terrible attitude. That was it.

You had to learn to separate the real people who were just fans or needed help from the foundation, from the scammers and the vulture types, and I sucked at it. Face to face, I've got you. But on the internet... I was horrible at reading people. Luckily Mikee just doesn't trust anyone at first, so she became the firewall. None of this would work without her.

Life with Sticky

Over the following months, everything became about the cat. People wanted to know how he was doing, what he was like, and to see updates we were more than happy to post. Who doesn't love cat photos?

One of the many we posted was of Sticky cuddling with Jojo. During this time, Jojo passed away peacefully, and people around the world mourned with us. We were receiving heartfelt messages about Jojo, with people remembering him in sweet ways. Anything that was monetary went to the Sticky the Kitty Foundation, but others were gifts, like a painting of that photo of Sticky and Jojo.

Everywhere we went, people asked about Sticky.

With the Foundation going smoothly, with Mikee running all of that, I suddenly found the ideas and inspiration to do what I'd always wanted to do: write children's books. It's a chance to reach kids when they're developing, and really help them when they're going through some things.

I knew a thing or two about some of those things kids go through or at least what I had gone through, and I knew what I wished I had heard as a child. I would write to the little 'Charlie's' of the world and there are a lot of little me's out there.

I suddenly had a giant audience, and kids absolutely loved hearing about Sticky. I'd met a guy during those first weeks named Max Marcel, who turned out to be an artist and who wanted to illustrate a children's book.

I'd send him a story, he'd send back illustrations, and they were perfect. It was better than I'd imagined, and I never had to correct him on anything.

It was another one of those things that felt like it was supposed to happen.

To this day, I still haven't actually spoken to him. All of our communication has been through Messenger or by email, and part of me finds that hilarious, but it just works. We've now done 6 books together, over 4 years, never speaking to each other. How did I get to this point? Oh, yeah... I found a cat.

My family got used to the weird cat fame pretty quickly and it all just settled into this all becoming normal life. The kids don't think twice about coming home to a news crew or a reporter anymore. It's just what happens in our house now.

Mikee did some of those interviews in the beginning, but quickly realized it wasn't for her. When I'd have early morning interviews, where the interview is on the East Coast, I'd have to be set up at 3 or 4am sometimes. She never got up, just let me do what I had to do.

Then, at her normal wake up time, Mikee would come out, sleepy-eyed to get her cup of coffee, and ask, "How's it going over there, superstar?" Then she'd give me a kiss and head back to our room to get on with her morning. She played agent, manager, editor, publisher, accountant, assistant and whoever else I needed through all of those first weeks of this adventure, as well as put together an entire foundation.

There's so much that wouldn't have happened without her involvement. But at the same time, she didn't want to be the face of the Foundation. She was more than happy working in the background and having me in front of the microphones, cameras, or whatever. Between us, it works, but again, I know it wouldn't work without her.

My 15-year-old twin boys think it's cool, but that's more because they can see how this helps people, and how much it means to so many people. If you asked them, they'd probably say that the moment in Sacramento, at the stoplight, has been one of the coolest, "dad is famous!" moments.

I've spoken at their school and they've gone to different events with me and are probably more well known on Stickys social media than they would like to be. Everyone knows their cat... it's just their life now. It's been fun for them, watching me either make a difference or be the goofiest guy in the world. I still haven't always figured out which is which, but the fact that they support me means the world.

Last Christmas, we had a news crew come by for the whole day, because they wanted to do segments at breakfast, lunch, and dinner on the books. Instead of packing up each time, they simply hung out with us.

My daughter and granddaughter were over, and my granddaughter was very curious about the proceedings. We got to talking with the reporter, who ended up answering my granddaughter's questions and having a pretty enlightening conversation with her.

My granddaughter looked at me. "So, they want you to do the show so people will watch it?"

"That's right," I said. "And I want to do the show so people will buy my books. So, we're kind of using each other. But nicely."

"That's exactly what's happening," the reporter said. "That's how these shows work. Your grandpa will bring people to our news show, and we will help him sell books. It sounds like we're using each other but we're all friends, so we're really helping each other."

She also told her, "You know a lot of the shows you see that are supposed to be 'reality shows', are never real. They are set up just like we set this all up." I was glad she told her that. My granddaughter was pretty enamored with this young, hip, television reporter and I think it was cool she heard that from her.

My granddaughter watched as we planned the filming of each segment, deciding when we would smile and pre-planning jokes, with her new inside knowledge of the entertainment business and was the perfect assistant as we got it all filmed. It was really cool to have her involved.

So often, we, and especially kids, think what we see on someone's social media accounts or on TV is their real life, when it's almost always manufactured for an audience. Once you understand that, it's much easier for some folks to enjoy their own situation a whole lot more.

The Downside to Fame

People look at me like I'm crazy when I tell them that fame isn't always that great. The moments are small, but

I think that if you don't have a good sense of yourself, it's easy for little negative moments to turn into big ones.

It's why my Grandma said it was a good thing I'd lost the fame I had as a teenager. I needed to grow more and experience life.

The sudden loss of anonymity can be a shock. I used to go to the grocery store, choose my items, pay, and leave. Within days after finding Sticky, that was gone. The produce section was now an adventure, not just a chore.

Don't get me wrong, I find it really cool to know that I mean so much to so many people, but it can be strange sometimes. Once in a while, you just want to melt into the background.

This lack of anonymity also means that I get those negative, mean comments. It's only one in thousands, but those are the ones you obsess over.

The first post about Sticky... there are now over a million likes and somewhere around three hundred thousand comments, and they're mostly talking about how they love me, or Sticky, or my family, talking about how much hope and joy it's brought them, to see this story unfold.

But the first negative comment about us or the books or something we have done... those are the ones you fixate on.

It's human nature. We want to be liked, and the first time we get a comment that definitely lets us know we're not, it bugs us. No matter how many happy and fun comments came before that one.

That's the thing about social media. It's easy to throw off a mean comment and be a jerk just to get at someone or freak them out. It's a lot easier to be mean than it would be in real life and there are very few consequences for it.

People do it because they get a thrill from it, or to give themselves a rush. Basically, making someone else feel bad makes them feel good. It's much easier to be a bully on social media than it is in real life, which means you encounter a lot more bullies.

Somehow you've got to learn how to ignore them, how to focus on the good things in life, on the beautiful comments and the words that lift you up. And that is a lesson for all of life. You can't spend your life upset about the one jerk.

One dead flower doesn't take away the beauty of an entire field. It's a hard lesson to learn, but an important one. If I'd run across this as a teen, it would have been tough and I'm sure it's tough for kids now. Face-to-face bullies were tough enough.

I feel for the kids today, and I hate hearing of some of the heavier consequences of social media bullying, but it's there, and I have heard the stories. I've talked to the parents of kids who aren't here anymore because that bullying became too much. I can't imagine. Kindness friends. We need more kindness.

Cat people can get very intense. You'll come across comments that say, "Oh, you rescued a cat? That's great! I have sixty-two cats!"

They'd send me a picture of their tiny, cat filled house, and all I can think is that has to smell terrible! Why would you DO that? I love cats but come on, man....

There are people who feel that because I've rescued a cat, and they're cat people, we should be best friends. It's been hard to explain and kind of disappointing to some people when I tell them I wasn't a 'cat rescuer' before I found Sticky.

I would have helped, you bet. I would have taken him home. And I did. But it wasn't my life. It was just my Friday morning that day. I just couldn't have 62 cats. I'm sorry to disappoint those folks but I'm at 3 and that's a lot, you know? 62? That's... well, you know, that's a different kind of cat person.

I know I've gotten thousands of friend requests and I wasn't great at dealing with that either. I accepted everyone at first, which turned out to be a bad idea. Mikee has gotten almost as many, but she doesn't respond unless I've known them for a couple of years, first. Very few folks have made it on to her list.

There are also different levels of fame. Especially in the internet age. The super fame is pretty fun. The mid-grade fame isn't as much fun. For the first few weeks, I was as famous as any famous person there was. Like I said, someone recognized me everywhere I went. I even had to take a week off of work, because a told a reporter where I worked and they used it in a story. People started showing up there, looking for me.

Mostly to just say thank you or to drop off a card, but when a guy waited for me at my car to tell me all about his cats, even show me photos, I realized I better take some time off and let this die down. How did he even know which car was mine?

This all happened just before Halloween and we already had a giant blow up cat decoration in our yard that we had been putting up for a couple of years. One photographer used it as a backdrop for one photo of Sticky and I, that made it around the world.

We had to take it down when a stranger on Facebook told us they knew where Silverton was and they would just look for the big cat balloon to drop by and say hi. It's been in a box in the garage ever since.

I had a guy that I refer to as Cousin Eddy question me, after realizing who I was, as to why I had translated one of my books into Spanish.

"Don't they have their own books?" Cousin Eddy asked.

"Yes, but they also have the same books we do. They're just in Spanish. We have some of theirs as well... you know, but in English." I tried to explain.

"They shouldn't get to have our books. They should have their own."

"And their own drinking fountains and bathrooms too?" I questioned, now annoyed by his obvious line of racist thinking.

Eddy shot me a look of ignorant fueled contempt, and then declared, "F*ck you."

I left him with, "You as well. Have a nice day." Kindness always wins.

I once passed a stranger as I was heading into a grocery store, and he was heading out. I saw him do the double take at me out of the corner of my eye as we passed each other, but I was on my lunch break, so I just tried to keep walking, pretending I hadn't seen him looking at me.

He stopped, turned in my direction and said loudly, "you know you aren't special? You aren't a hero." I understood that label being used on me, for what I did, may upset some folks who knew actual war heroes or that kind of thing, so I turned and said, "I know. I'm not the one who said I was."

He reiterated as if I maybe hadn't heard him the first time, "You aren't special. You didn't do anything." For whatever reason, that second time hit me wrong. I knew I wasn't special, and I had never said I was. In fact, all I had said was that I wasn't.

But this guy and I didn't know each other. I understood what he was saying, but I just couldn't let the rudeness of it pass.

I took a step towards him. "What have you done to make the world even a little bit better? Anything?" I asked. He stepped back a step or two, eyes widened and stunned. Again, but this time much quieter, he said, "You aren't a hero."

"That's what I thought", I responded, my finger still pointing at his face and I walked into the store. I probably didn't handle that as well as I could have, but when do random strangers tell you how not special you are? When you're cat famous, that's when.

After things die down, your level of fame changes to a different kind of uncomfortable. You are still noticed, but it's not like it was in those first days of it all. If you knew me, you knew me and if you didn't.. you still felt like you might.

People look at you like they know you but can't quite remember where from. It could be TV... or it could be the office Christmas party. They kind of smile and do a sort of point thing in a gesture of, "Don't I know you?"

I know where you probably know me from, but what if I'm wrong? I'll sound crazy talking about my cat, which has happened.

I once stood in a line as two women stood behind me, whispering. I heard one ask the other, "is that him?" so I turned around. They both smiled and one asked me if "he" was as cute in real life as he seemed. I told them he was kind of a jerk but someone had glued him to a road so you couldn't blame him.

Their expressions both went blank, and I realized they did not know what I was talking about or who my cat was. They asked if I was Andy, and I asked if they meant Sticky and suddenly their excitement turned to annoyance that I had pretended to be Andy. To this day, I still don't know who Andy was.

I tried to explain, but at that point you just sound creepier. See the difference between being the cool cat guy for those kids in traffic, and a creepy guy telling you about a cat glued to a road? It's not nearly as much fun being that second guy. And there I was thinking I could pull off being, Andy...

You begin to look at people differently as well. Why is that person looking at me? Do they know me and or am I supposed to know them? Do they want to talk to me about Sticky or do I have something in my teeth? I don't want to be the weird guy, but what if this person genuinely just wants to say hi?

After a few missed cues and mistaken cat stories told, you begin to not engage as much with people. It's just easier and helps avoid a lot of embarrassment, but it also comes off as snooty. Then you're snooty. Cat fame can be a tough balancing act.

The hardest thing about it all, the one that's been the most difficult to accept, are the friends I've lost.

When this all happened, within weeks my friends split into two camps: "This is so cool!" or "This is ridiculous." And it was all over the 'cat thing,' which is how the friends who left referred to me finding a cat.

I could almost pick who would land in which camp based on how long they'd known me.

While I became known as The Cat Guy, more and more of my newer friends, some of the ones I'd made since moving to Oregon, started getting irritated. They were fed up with 'the cat thing' and with me talking about the things we were doing because of Sticky, like the children's books or the Foundation. Even when they were the ones to ask about it. When I would run into them, they had this look of almost pity. It was a look that kind of said, "awww... he thinks he can do something with his life."

I once pointed out to a coworker that my first book was on the same page of a website as a Dr. Seuss book. They were quick to point out that the font about my book was much smaller than it was for the Dr. Seuss book. Sure... it's Dr. Seuss... It was things like that all the time. So many of them were so quick to poo-poo anything we were trying to do. I eventually stopped talking with these friends about it, even though it was the main thing happening in our lives at the time.

It's interesting how the groups seemed to split. A lot of these newer friends, that had met me at an older age after I had moved to Oregon, had an image of me in their heads. I was the head of maintenance at a local Silverton resort for a few years, then the Director of Maintenance at The Salvation Army. They knew me as the HVAC guy, the maintenance man who would play some music and talk about surfing.

That's it.

It was like that's all they wanted me to be. They didn't want to hear me talking about kindness and being cool to each other. They couldn't accept that I was never just the maintenance man. That was just what I did. It wasn't who I was. But something at this point in my life made it hard for people to see me as anything other than that maintenance guy.

A lot of them were so over the cat thing and what they thought they were watching me do, that they were completely missing the bigger picture. They missed what Sticky meant to people on a much deeper level. They just saw the surface and thought I was trying to be more than I should be.

The guy I am now, the one who writes children's books, speaks at schools, and talks about kindness and how we are ALL someone is so much more of who I really am, than the small object in the tiny box they wanted me to stay in.

Because that's what it was. They wanted me to stay inside a little box where they could give me one or two labels. They didn't want to get to know all the parts of me, or to accept them.

The people who had known me as a younger man were excited at this new life that was unfolding in front of me and could easily see me being all of those things. I heard more than once from that group that I was the perfect person to spread this message.

I frequently heard nothing from that new group. When those friends started turning away, it seemed like it was a matter of, "you can't be this kind cat guy because you're the middle-aged maintenance man." Why can't I be both?

We tend to develop a perception of who people are based on what they do when you first meet them, especially after a certain age. The trick is whether you're able to see that they are more than their job, or what 'they do'. We are all so much more than what we do for a living or who we love or even who we pray to.

I don't believe anyone is just a "_____". We are all something very special. I also know how much easier it is to say that, than it is to believe it sometimes. I've been there.

My older friends, the ones who had known me for years and who were never anything but excited to hear what we were up to - the ones who were never anything but supportive - were the ones I should have been focusing on that entire time. They are the beautiful field, to those couple dead flowers.

Recently, I saw one of those newer friends, someone I'd worked with for years and who I'd talk to daily. She was across the street, walking down the sidewalk. I don't know if she saw me. I wanted to call out, to get her attention, but I hesitated.

Did she even want to talk to me? After all, she'd been one of the first in the "this is ridiculous" camp. And while I thought about it, she passed, and my chance was gone. I really miss our conversations, but when she asked what I had been up to, what am I gonna say? Then, when I say it, what look is she going to give me? I guess if it's between our conversations and the hope and kindness that's spreading because I stopped for a kitten, I'll have to take the hope every time.

5

BELINDA LAND

Belinda Land

I only knew Belinda Land for a brief time, but I can't imagine that I will ever forget her.

In early 2019, I received an award from the Humane Society called The Diamond Collar Hero Award. According to their website, they give the award to people or pets that have shown 'extraordinary compassion, commitment, and kindness.'

It was a very humbling honor, albeit a little uncomfortable. We were a few months into the 'hero' thing and my friends were pretty firmly planted in those two camps. Receiving an award called the Diamond Collar Hero Award would bring none of the 'this is ridiculous' camp back into the circle.

Never the less, it was still a very cool honor, and I was proud to receive it.

There was an award ceremony attached to receiving this award, held at an exclusive racket club in Portland, Oregon. They had a luncheon to attend, a bunch of speeches, and then, of course, the awards. I was one of four and I was excited to attend and see what all of this was about.

Being award recipients, we didn't have to buy our tickets, but I would find out later it was $50 a ticket to attend the ceremony.

When we arrived, we had to check in at the front desk. Sticky was with us, looking at everything and sometimes trying to escape.

At the desk, the receptionist smiled. "Your friend Belinda has already arrived. She'll be sitting with you at lunch today."

I stared at her, confused. "Belinda? I don't know any Belinda."

"Well, she seems to know you.", the woman said.

Life moved on, I did a couple of quick interviews, but the whole time, I can't help but wonder if I'd met a Belinda and simply forgotten about it. The truth is, I'm terrible with names. It's one reason I call everyone 'brother' or 'sister.' I rarely remember people's names, but I really should, and I don't want to admit I've forgotten. Again.

As hard as I tried, I couldn't think of a Belinda from anywhere in our life. I was about to get a Belinda in my life.

A family saw us and came over, the kids smiling but a little shy. "You're the cat guy!" their dad said, reaching out to shake my hand.

"Yep, that's me."

"And Sticky!"

I held him up for them to see, but Sticky is understandably uncomfortable with strangers, so a quick pat is all he allows.

"Is it all right if we take a picture with you two?" the dad asked.

"Yeah, you bet." I smiled. I love seeing kids get so excited by something that's so easy for me to give.

They passed their phone to a bystander, and we posed, but right before the camera clicked, a woman off to the side shouted, "Chuck! Chuck! Chuck!"

I've never seen the picture, but I imagine all of us were staring off to the side, trying to find the freight train barreling down towards us. A tiny blonde woman raced down the hallway, waving, a huge smile on her face. She stopped next to the person taking our picture, nearly vibrating while she waited for us to finish.

The father and I thanked each other for each other's time as this excited, tiny woman hopped in place like a child meeting Santa for the first time. Turning my attention from the family to her, I smiled.

"Hi!"

"Oh, my God!" She rushed over, hugging me tightly. I looked down at her, surprised, but patted her back. When she stepped back, she smiled brightly. "I'm Belinda!"

"Oh, okay." I laughed. "You're Belinda!"

"Yes!" she bounced, clapping her hands. "I can't believe I'm finally meeting you and Sticky! I love your story. It changed my whole life..."

Mikee came over, saving me from what had become a very familiar story that folks always felt they needed to share. Another humbling but slightly uncomfortable situation I was having to learn to deal with. I knew what I did, and it was something many people have done. I found a cat. How this time had changed people's lives was still a bit of a mystery to me.

We spent the luncheon with Belinda, who had taken a day off work to be there, but also paid for two seats in order to sit with us. I stared at her, astonished, when she told us that, but she turned out to be the sweetest lady. Normally I'd be very uncomfortable in that situation, subjected to what amounted to hero worship.

"It's like meeting Brad and Angelina!" she gushed. Silly yes, but to make someone that happy just by sitting with them... that's an easy win.

Because of her sweet nature and general bubbly look at life, it all became a really fun thing, never awkward or weird. We really enjoyed spending the luncheon with her.

As a human award recipient, they asked me to address the room, and telling them how I'd spoken to my supervisor a few weeks before finding Sticky seemed to flow naturally.

"I even told him 'I want to give people hope.'" I told the crowd. "But Oprah's got that gig already." That got a good laugh. "I thought I didn't know too many other people who could work 'hope' as a career. Maybe it's not a career but something to work to achieve." The speech went well, and I returned to our table with my new crystal trophy in hand. It was a cool moment.

There were four Diamond Collar Hero Awards given out that day, and one of them was to a therapy llama, Rojo. I could not get over this, and I kept wandering away to talk to the owners and pet Rojo. I've heard of therapy dogs, ponies, and even a few cats, but a llama?

He was a very sweet llama, and I was a little more comfortable spending time with him than with the groups of strangers wanting to talk to us and meet Sticky. It seemed that Rojo and I were the stars of the 2019 Awards, and I was more than happy to hang out with the llama.

Belinda watched all this with delight, just talking about how excited she was to be there with us and meet us. I got the sense that her life might be kind of tough, but she was so kind and looked at everything with joy and hope.

When we parted at the end of the luncheon, we exchanged emails to stay in touch. Two weeks after the event, she sent me a small stuffed llama that sits on my desk to this day. It was one of the most thoughtful gifts anybody has ever sent me.

Over the next year, Belinda continued to support everything we did, from donating to the Sticky the Kitty Foundation to buying multiple copies of every children's book I put out. She was one of the first to buy a Sticky doll and the first one to send me a photo of her doll, out traveling with her, starting what would become a 'thing' with lots of Sticky doll adoptees.

We kept in touch through Facebook and emails, and I usually signed off by calling her 'Sister.' Simply a habit from my difficulty in remembering names. Who have I talked to recently, who am I talking to now... I know why we're talking, and what we're talking about, but names... man!

A little over a year after we met, I received a message from her. She was in the hospital in Vancouver, WA; she was sick; they didn't know what it was; they thought it might be cancer, but she wasn't sure. Could I come visit her?

That made me pause because I hadn't felt we'd known each other like that. We'd only met the one day for a couple of hours. She was super cool and very supportive of our business, but I would have thought she'd want family around her, not a near stranger like me.

I thought about that one for a while, finally deciding that even though I didn't feel like we were that close, she did, and she needed someone to be with her.

The next day, I took a long lunch and drove just over the border to Vancouver.

As I walked into Belinda's room, a couple sitting directly across from the door stood up. A curtain stretched across half the room, hiding Belinda.

The couple smiled. "Have you come to see Belinda?" the man asked.

"Hi. Yeah. I'm Chuck... Chuck Hawley."

Despite the heaviness in the room, they brightened a bit more. "She's been waiting for you," the woman said as they stepped past me to leave.

"You guys don't have to go," I said.

"We'll just give you some privacy and stretch our legs."

I walked around the curtain to see Belinda sitting up in bed, wearing a hospital gown. She didn't look sick. She had the same bright smile from the Awards ceremony, but I could see the fear in her eyes.

I'd like to say I was comfortable in that role. I wish I could say that all came naturally to me, but the truth is the whole situation was so strange to me. The heaviness in the room, being asked to sit at the bedside of someone who was nearly a stranger to me, but who themselves, felt so close to me at the same time.

I took a deep breath and smiled, as I sat at the foot of her bed. "What's up, sister? When are they letting you out of here?"

Her smile faded a little. She had none of her usual spring. Her feet, covered in purple socks with little rubber paw prints on the bottom, stuck out the end of her blanket next to me.

Without thinking, I began rubbing her feet, then nearly stopped when I realized what I was doing. But she relaxed a little, so I kept it up.

"I don't know." Her voice shook slightly. Frustrated, she leaned forward, trying to see around the curtain as if trying not to get caught complaining about the doctors. "They're not telling me anything. Well, almost nothing. They've said I might have Stage 4 liver cancer. It's been two days since then and no news."

She talked about her cat, and how worried she was about what would happen to him if something happened to her.

I couldn't believe this. She's been stuck in a hospital for two days with no news? What kind of crazy is all this? She stopped talking abruptly when a doctor came into the room. He took her vitals, so I sat back in the chair to give him space.

She looked up at him, and asked, "Am I going to die?"

He just smiled at her while he continued to work.

"Am I going to die?" she asked again, this time asking more forcefully.

"We need to get the test results back before we can give you any answers," he said, obviously refusing to commit to anything.

I stared at her, dumbfounded by the non-answer from the doctor, as he left the room. When you ask a question like that, you expect a doctor to say something reassuring. Anything.

"That's all they'll say to me," she cried, big tears rolling down her cheeks.

I moved back to the foot of the bed to resume the foot rub. "Okay, well... he didn't say anything yet. Don't freak out. Don't go there. No news is good news until it isn't." I rambled through all the cliches you can think of to say in a moment like that.

She immediately started talking about her cat again. "You'll take care of him, won't you?"

"We'll find him a good home, but it won't be necessary. You're going to be okay." I smiled at her, but before I could say more, another man walked through the door.

Dressed in casual clothes, he came in and flopped down in a chair next to Belinda's bed with such easy familiarity I assumed he was another friend. Belinda seemed a little uncomfortable, but I put that down to the situation and just seeing the doctor. I moved back to the chair. Meeting her friend should be interesting.

"So, how are you doing today?" he asked.

"I don't know!" Belinda said, an edge of panic in her voice. "They're not giving me any answers."

"They haven't told you anything?"

"No."

"Oh." He sat back, surprised. "Okay..." He looked down the bed, finally noticing me at the foot. "Hi."

"Hey," I said. "I'm Chuck."

"Nice to meet you, Chuck. I'm Chaplain Richards. I'm one of the hospital chaplains."

Oh, shit!

Now, I didn't have much experience with this kind of thing, but it seemed to me that having a chaplain come visit when you're in the hospital without answers isn't a great sign.

He turned back to Belinda. "You know, Belinda, there are worse things than death," he said.

My jaw dropped. How do you say that to someone who's already scared and in that position, who isn't being given any information on her condition? I'm sure it was somehow meant to be comforting, but it was not.

By the time I could pay attention again, he was smiling. "Well, I'll leave you to it, Belinda, and I'll see what I can find out for you."

He squeezed her hand, nodded to me, and breezed out like he'd brought her a basket of sunshine. We sat staring at each other with the words, "There are worse things than death," floating like smoke, thick in the air of that small hospital room.

She just looked horrified.

My mind began racing. A combination of her horror, my anger at him for saying that, and both of our sadness as I searched for anything to say to make that moment better for her. "Listen, that guy doesn't know what he's talking about. What an ass. I can't believe he just said that. Don't listen to him, sister. He's not a doctor, he doesn't know anything." I'm trying to think of a story, anything, to distract her, and I just have nothing.

In Belinda's eyes, all I could see was this incredible fear, the kind most of us can't even comprehend.

The alarm on my phone went off, telling me I needed to go back to work, but I didn't move. It was just a surreal moment. We sat in silence, just staring at each other for what seemed like hours, although it was probably just a few minutes before her friends came back into the room.

"I'm sorry, but I have to go back to work," I said.

She took my hand. "Will you come back and visit me again?"

"Of course I will, sister." I leaned down, hugging her tightly. "Don't give up."

She gave me a shaky smile. "Sticky didn't. I won't, either."

"Atta girl."

I left smiling, and as upbeat as I could be, telling her I would see her later.

But safely in my car, it was so different. I sat there for several minutes, exhausted. I cried a bit. Being this new person, someone who brought hope, carried a heavy responsibility I hadn't had to deal with before.

I wasn't a guru or a priest or a therapist. I just found a kitten. But I had asked the universe to let me give people hope. I had asked to be this person. I had rubbed that lamp and my wish had been granted. While I hadn't expected to be this particular person, I was grateful I could be whatever person Belinda needed in that moment.

She had been so supportive of us and our projects. She was such a fan of our cat. A cat she had only met once at an awards ceremony, but who she now found strength in. This cat and I were giving her hope.

So, yeah, no matter how draining it might be emotionally, I'd be there for her.

Two days later, Belinda was released from the hospital. She had Stage 4 liver cancer, and it had spread to her bones. The doctors were planning a treatment regimen for her, but she didn't know how long she'd have if the treatment didn't work.

We messaged Daily. Belinda filling me in on what treatment they were trying, or I'd just check in, asking her how she was feeling. She lived in Chehalis, Washington, which was a good drive away. I had planned on going up and taking Sticky to see her.

I just never got the chance.

About two weeks after I visited her in the hospital, on February 26, 2020, I received a text from Belinda. It simply read, Thank you so much. It's nice to know I have a big brother.

I didn't know in what context she was sending this text, so I simply responded, 'Always', with a heart emoji.

I messaged her over the next three days, but heard nothing back. When I finally got a response, it was one of Belinda's friends, using her phone. Belinda's health had taken a turn for the worse, and she was back in the hospital.

When can I go see her? I texted back. Maybe I could sneak this cat into the hospital for her. Anything to make her feel better.

But the next message nearly broke me.

'The doctors don't think she'll make it through the day.' the first text read.

What can you say to that? I think I said 'Okay,' but that didn't come anywhere close to expressing how I truly felt about it.

'When they brought her in, all she wanted to bring with her was her Sticky doll,' they said next.

Just her Sticky doll. I couldn't respond.

I spent the rest of my day in a daze, waiting for—and dreading—another message. It came that evening.

'Belinda passed away this afternoon. She was holding her Sticky doll when she passed. Thank you for being there for her. You made a big difference in her life.'

This little spitfire of a woman who had come bouncing into our lives a year and some change before was gone.

She had made an incredible impression on my life, and I on hers. Somehow this little cat and I were able to give her some hope when she needed it most, and then a little comfort as she left this world. Maybe this cat really is an angel.

Belinda Land, you will not be forgotten.

6

PEOPLE FROM ALL WALKS OF LIFE

People from all walks of life

As this Sticky train got rolling, I began to meet people from all over the world. From every corner and walk of life, you could think of. It started locally and then quickly spread out throughout the country. Every type of person you could think of began reaching out to me.

I met coal miners, teachers, politicians, doctors, police officers, therapists, celebrities, pastors and priests, dancers, truck drivers, pilots, writers and directors, grandmas and grandpas, aunts and uncles, and just about everyone else you could think of. People love cats. There is something magical about cats and people who have little else in common, found common ground in this kitten. I also met a lot of *real* heroes. Folks, who you may or may not have ever heard of, but all honest to goodness heroes, in their own way.

What started to become apparent about these different folks from all of these different walks of life was that they were all so much more similar than they were different. Sure, they had different jobs and different daily lives, different ideologies often, but they all basically wanted the same thing. To be happy.

That's true for the shopkeeper from Bangladesh, all the way to the grandma from Ohio. No matter where you started or where you ended up, you want to be happy. You want your family and friends to be happy. Living creatures, and that means all living creatures, want to be happy. That often starts with kindness. To deny something or someone that happiness is pretty unkind, right?

Being a natural introvert, it was amazing to have conversations with people I normally wouldn't have talked to from interesting places that I probably would have never gone to. I pretty quickly found myself talking to folks from Europe, Australia, Africa, Pakistan.... places I would have *never* been able to go. It was like the world had opened up to me. I had invitations to sleep on couches all over the planet. Had I not been a dad, and husband with responsibilities, I would have absolutely gone on a world, couch surfing tour. Maybe someday.

In talking to my new friends in Africa, I found a kind of joy that you don't find everywhere. It was a kind of pure happiness that just emanated light and kindness. So much dancing and singing. So much celebrating of nature and the world and just the magic that is life. They are beautiful people to visit with.

I met a man who you may have seen on the web or television, by the name of Patrick Sadiki. He is a park ranger in the Virunga National Park in the Congo. He protects gorillas from poachers. As in, he has actual gun fights with poachers who are trying to kill and sell the gorillas of the park. In the short time I have known him, he has lost two of his fellow park rangers in those gun fights. He still exudes that joy the Africans seem to be born with.

I have so much fun talking with Australians. They also have a lot of joy but it's a different joy than the Africans. It seems you have to be a certain kind of tough to live in some places in Australia and the sense of humor that comes with that kind of life is awesome! We met a woman named Kellie who lived in the outback. She would send us photos of these dinosaur like lizards that would creep into her house. I suppose you either laugh or scream. They do a lot of laughing down there.

We had a fan club of rugby players for a while. They blew up that picture of Sticky sitting on my shoulder and set it up... wherever rugby players hang out. When they were through training and ready to relax, they'd sit around it and drink a beer with Sticky and I, toasting us and setting a beer down in front of our picture. I'm humbled and honored to be included, although I don't think I'm nearly tough enough to live down there.

I made friends with people from many European countries as well. I had some amazing conversations about the history of their respective countries, their daily lives, their music and culture, their public figures, and even their own countries' celebrity pets. They've all got their own, 'Stickys'. I learned some Italian, some Swedish, a little German and some Spanish. Pegajoso El Gatito (Sticky the Kitty)

I suddenly had access to people from all over the world. I spent hours just talking to people online and learning about their lives and places most of us have never even heard of. It was amazing.

At one point, I somehow got connected to a woman from Syria while they were in the middle of a civil war. Somehow she had heard about Sticky and just wanted to reach out and say thank you. She was a teacher and had told her students about Sticky's story. We talked off and on for a week or so, with her telling me about daily shelling and having to teach kids in underground bunkers and just the life that goes on while living in an active civil war, in a modern city.

They would have certain times of day when they could go to the store, when they knew the shelling would be lighter. That a store was even open shows you the strength of the human spirit. When the water would be shut off, they would go to broken pipes they knew about that constantly ran. This apparently happened often. You had to boil everything. But you rarely had power or gas. So you made camp fires.

These were modern people, in a modern city, making the best of a situation they had no control over. *That* is the kind of thing I was suddenly learning about first hand. They were amazing but sometimes heartbreaking conversations. I'm reading these messages as my children are safe and fed and just worried about who said what to who at school today. I couldn't help but feel like I knew these Syrian kids.

We made plans for me to send her and her students some books, but she suddenly stopped responding. The end of her messages coincided with news reports of a chemical weapons attack over there. It's a horrible feeling to think about the reasons she may have stopped responding, but it is a reality of the world that most of us are so sheltered from. I just hope she and those kids are okay out there somewhere.

I met a lovely woman named Annie from Colorado. Annie had a property with rental cabins high in the Rockies after enduring incredible loss. She had lost two of her children when they were both very young. Several years later, she lost her husband to depression. She had been a life flight nurse in a helicopter and somehow survived a horrible crash that left her with her own PTSD.

Despite all of this, she sent me the most beautiful photos of snow-covered mountains, and elk and wild animals that came to visit her property. Even through these horrible tragedies, she found beauty all around her every day. And I have been so humbled that she has shared that beauty with me.

Reminder time again: This is all happening to a 'maintenance guy' who stopped for a kitten on the road. Kindness will take you to some amazing places... Ok, back to the story.

I met a woman and her niece from Ireland. The most beautiful and gentle souls, Madonna and Macie Jane. Both avid animal lovers and wonderful people. Macie was the first person from another country that I heard reading one of my books. To hear my book read by a little girl in Ireland, in her natural, beautiful Irish accent, is an incredible feeling.

Speaking of cool accents, I also met a young Mr. Jack Strain from Worcester, UK. Mr. Strain and his family sent me a video of him showing off his newly learned reading skills using one of my books. A right proper lad with a right proper British name, reading one of my books with his right proper British accent. Also another very proud and humbling moment for me and I was so happy to share it with Mr. Strain. That was a good day.

As I mentioned earlier, the first children's book is translated into Spanish. That was done by a Spanish III class as their final exam in a Christian High School in Pennsylvania. Their teacher, Jacqueline, made that all happen out of the kindness of her heart and a love for the Sticky story. That class ended up going on a mission to the Dominican Republic, so we donated several copies of that Spanish version of the book and a bunch of Sticky dolls for them to take to an orphanage.

Pakistan

Pakistan is a rough and brutal existence. Even in the good parts. I got to have a little more hands on approach when we got to Pakistan.

About two years before writing this book, someone ordered some books for an orphanage in Pakistan. I sent the books, and I ended up receiving an email, thanking me for the books. They also sent a picture. In it, the children were sitting on the ground—a concrete floor—there's four brick walls around them, a doorway, and spaces for windows but... no roof.

The children are reading the books I'd sent, but I kept looking at the space where a roof should be. So, I messaged Sumeera and Victor—the people caring for the kids in the orphanage—back, asking about the missing roof. I was really just interested to know what kind of building they were sitting inside.

Victor replied, telling me it was their school. Since they had little funds, they couldn't build it all at once. Instead, they built when they had the money to do so.

Okay... "How much does a roof cost to build in Pakistan?" I messaged back.

He said it would cost $4,000 to build.

I thought about this one for a few days, figuring some things out, before I got back to him. *If I can get you the money, can you coordinate building the roof?*

Being the resourceful sort you have to be to survive in Pakistan, Victor said he could do that. A construction project in Pakistan is not like a construction project in the US.

There are no Home Depots, but somehow Victor pulled together crews and materials as we figured out how to get it paid for.

We began fundraising through Sticky's people, talking to everyone we knew, and posting both on Sticky's page and on my profile. With many people's help and generosity, we raised more than what they needed to put a roof on this little orphanage and we began a construction project halfway around the world.

Mikee and I now had our actual jobs, a nonprofit foundation to run, children's books being written and sent out, multiple charity side projects going on, not to mention our daily lives, kids and animals. It seemed like we had a full plate. So we just added another plate somewhere. This had just become our life.

I sent the money over in parts, as we received it, and they began building. Victor would send me daily pictures of their progress and we began a construction project on the opposite side of the planet. The things people can achieve when they are doing something with the intent of bettering people's lives is astounding, and it was amazing to be a part of, even if it was in just a small way from the other side of the planet.

It took us a bit of time, but they got it finished up before the rainy season hit. A roofless building in the 'rainy season' of Pakistan is basically a swimming pool. Not the ideal place to conduct school lessons.

The Pakistani people are incredibly resourceful. They have very little compared to many in the world, but they make it work. Even they can only do so much without a roof during the torrential downpours they get during monsoon season. Victor did an outstanding job.

With the extra money we had raised, they put in lights and fans and fully wired the building. Now, they don't just use it as a school; it doubles as a community center for their town. One of the regular groups to use it is a group that teaches women the skills necessary to be more independent. There are several types of classes running there. I don't know how many they have now, but I know it is heavily used.

When the school had been completed, Victor and Sumeera sent us a photo of the kids, each with a coloring page. I have boxes of pictures of these kids with Sticky coloring book pages. It's awesome.

During the entire building process, I learned more about the kids. When we first began writing, I asked where these kids were from, and the answers broke my heart. They're street kids, mostly.

A very few of them would sleep at the school—which Victor and Sumeera preferred—but most of them couldn't understand sleeping in one place and felt more comfortable with the streets. It was known and familiar. They'd live in groups, and go to school during the day, where they'd be educated, clothed, and, most importantly, to those kids... fed.

Are they all orphans? Where are their parents? I asked.

This one turned out to be a complicated question.

They didn't have parents, but not all of their parents were dead. Some were dead, but others had just disappeared. Some were born to slaves and other's parents had sold themselves into slavery to pay off debts. This is today. Not 200 years ago. There are people in this world that are selling themselves into slavery to pay off their debts. Let that sink in for a minute. For those kids whose parents had died,

Pakistan doesn't currently have a well-functioning social system to care for orphaned children.

Then, who takes care of them?

Victor explained that on the street, the five-year-old takes care of the four-year-old. The six-year-old takes care of the five-year-old, and the seven-year-old takes care of the six-year-old and so on. In one photo was what looked like a toddler, three or four years old, cooking in a wok. This little kid had a fire going under it, pouring oil, and stirring a rice mixture.

The child seemed quite at home but I couldn't help thinking that I'd have a hard time letting a nine-year-old touch a hot pan, much less a toddler. They didn't know anything different. This is just how it was.

The craziest thing is that if that three-year-old had gotten burned, it would have been the four-year-old trying to bandage him up. Can you even imagine?

My first instinct is to call it very *Lord of the Flies,* except that's not right. In *The Lord of the Flies,* those kids went crazy. These kids are *caring* for each other to the best of their abilities. They're showing... I don't know if it's love, yet, but it's solidarity, an understanding that they can't make it alone.

Call it community, maybe.

And all Victor and Sumeera can do is care for any and all children who show up at their door.

When Victor and Sumeera first sent me pictures of these kids, none of them were smiling. When I asked why not, they said the kids didn't know if they were supposed to. They said the kids would smile if I wanted them to.

If I wanted them to?! I wanted them... Oh my gosh; I wanted so much for them. I wanted them to have homes, to be fed, and cared for. Not being able to hand them those things, all I wanted was to know if they were happy. So I said, *"If they're happy, I want them to smile."*

In the next picture I received, all the kids were smiling. You could see how genuine they were, how much they loved having a roof and some coloring pages and just being able to be a kid. But think about that for a minute. They wouldn't show any expression until and unless they knew it was okay. Victor and Sumeera give them a sanctuary where it is okay to smile, in a part of our world where it can be very hard to find something to smile about.

Victor and Sumeera are some of the more inspirational people I have met along this journey. There are countless kids who literally wouldn't survive if it weren't for Victor and his wife. In the world they live in, those poor children's bodies would just be something else to step over or move off the road.

While what they do for those kids is incredible, it's not just the kids. It's whole villages of people. During the Covid pandemic, I saw photos of Victor delivering food to sick villagers, stuck in lock downs, never worrying about himself. I've seen him hanging off the back of motorcycles, weaving in and out of traffic on dusty Pakistani roads, to deliver medicine to people. During recent historic flooding over there, Victor was once again in the middle of it all, saving anyone that happened to cross his path. I'd bet a lot of you have never heard of Mr. Victor Gulzar or his wife Sumeera, but Victor and Sumeera are the walking, talking definition of heroes.

Their whole life is about caring for others in a place where it is very hard to care about anything other than how you survive that day, yourself. They are kindness personified and I might add two more that I have no doubt are angels.

Did you know... I'm an official Girl Scout?

After my second book, I received a letter from Girl Scout Troop 2045.

Hi Mr. Chuck!

My name is Elsie and I am in Girl Scout Troop 2045 in Illinois. We wanted to tell you that you were being a very good Girl Scout when you saved Sticky. You also write very good books and we read them at our meetings. We voted and we would like to tell you that you are officially a GIRL SCOUT! You do all the things to be a good Girl Scout and your books do, too.

Congratulations! Love you so much!

Troop 2045

I was so stoked when I received that letter. The day my sash came in was a bigger day than I could have ever imagined it would be. I was really proud. I'm a fifty-two year old man, and I'm proud to say that I am a real Girl Scout.

Don't think a 'Troop 2045' tattoo isn't in the plans. It's coming.

Elsie and her family have become some of my favorite people on this ride. Elsie has been one of the absolute biggest supporters of the kids' books. I am not kidding when I say she has been the reason I have kept going during some of my more frustrating days of trying to make a career out of writing.

It seems just about the time I have been ready to give up, I've gotten some kind of note from Elsie or a photo from her mom showing Elsie reading my books to a class or to OUR Girl Scout troop. It just takes one person sometimes, and Elsie has been that one many times. Another Angel? Maybe...

Other folks—often teachers—have reached out, talking about how they've used my books to help teach their kids. Everyone is unique in how they use my books, but the one thing they tell me is that the kids really relate to and love them.

This is one of my favorites and the letter that started those conversations in Africa.

To Mr. Chuck Hawley,

My name is Lucy Swayngin. I am a teacher and a counselor to our students at the Kagongo Primary School in Kenya, Africa.

I think you must know you are very famous in Kenya. I want to thank you for writing books of compassion and love. For our young men to see such a man as yourself show compassion to God's creatures is a great gift to us in our teaching.

We have two Sticky books used in our classrooms and also for when a child needs to learn compassion. They must read this before returning to the group.

Thank you, sir, and please tell me of future books.

Lucy Swayngin

They also use them to teach the children English. As an author, this whole letter lets me know I'm on the right track and to hear it from as far away as Kenya... I can't describe that feeling. Each one of these messages is the best review I could ever ask for.

Another one of my favorites is from a therapist in North Carolina, USA.

Hi, Chuck.

I wanted to let you know how I use your story book, A Sticky Situation, *frequently in my work as a licensed professional counselor and play therapist.*

I read the story with each child as a way to introduce "sticky things can happen" but we can work our way through them. Then, we make a batch of slime and we talk about the sticky situations in their lives—like Sticky's glue. Then, as we add the ingredients to make the slime more manageable, we talk about ways out of the sticky situations in their lives.

The children really seem to get it and it's fun to share the stories with them.

Thank you for sharing your and Sticky's stories and know you are helping many others with their own sticky situations.

There's an aunt who sent me a message, talking about how these books comforted her nieces while their parents were going through a nasty divorce. The older one, eleven years old at the time, said, "If Sticky can survive what happened to him, I can, too."

That was another crying moment. Those kids had a rough time of it, and they found comfort with Sticky. The last I heard, life had settled down for them, thankfully. All I wanted to do was give people hope. I'm grateful that wish came true.

I never imagined any of this happening, and if I had tried, I couldn't have dreamed of all the different ways people would relate to Sticky.

Ciella

Ciella is seven years old. She's a special one.

Last year, right before Christmas, Ciella lost her mom, Sara, to an undiagnosed medical condition. Her mom was only in her 20s, and like Belinda, it just shouldn't have happened.

Little Ciella, only six years old, had to go live with her grandparents.

Ciella's aunt, Pam, has been a Sticky fan since the beginning. Pam sent me a note, telling me a little of Ciella's story, then she ordered some books and asked if I would write Ciella a note in one of the books.

We began talking more, and as the story unfolded, we knew Christmas would not be a good one for Ciella. We got the Sticky fans together, and we did our best to do something special for her. Ciella was a fan of a particular doll, and we got her one of every version available, and we added the Sticky doll because... well, Sticky's helped a lot of people. Maybe some of his magic would help Ciella, too.

Ciella ended up latching onto the Sticky doll, although it took a while before I realized how much.

I got a note somewhere along the line that Ciella wanted a Sticky birthday. By that, I mean Sticky themed balloons, streamers, paper plates, the works. We couldn't pull that one off for her. We don't have *any* of those things.

I had not had this request yet, though. What this really did was to bring home how much Sticky meant to this little girl, but I still didn't quite understand just how much yet.

Pam and I continued to correspond, and one spring day, she sends me a picture of Ciella in the emergency room with a bandage around her hand, lying on a bed, waiting to go into surgery! Her Sticky doll was lying next to her.

Ciella was having a really terrible year. I asked Pam what had happened. She told me how Ciella's grandpa had been trimming the bushes with a hedge trimmer. Ciella reached up to help and caught her fingertips in the machine.

I felt horrible for Ciella, but I felt horrible for grandpa too. Grandpa does a lot for that family out there and I'm sure that was just as bad a day for him as it was for Ciella.

Pam assured me Ciella was doing well, and the next day, I got another message that she was recovering nicely. The hospital staff had let her take Sticky into surgery with her and suddenly, the entire surgery staff and all the nurses knows about Sticky and his story.

At the start of the school year, Ciella began second grade. It turns out the Sticky doll and Ciella's new teacher had a bit of a run in.

I learned all of this in a story her grandma, Penny, posted on Facebook. She was upset at how the teacher handled the entire situation, which, as I was told, goes like this:

During the first week of school, Penny gets a phone call from Ciella's new teacher. "Ciella has brought a toy to school. I don't know if you are aware, but we have a rule, no toys allowed in the classroom. She can collect it at the end of the day, but if she brings it again, I will keep it for the rest of the year."

Penny asked the teacher what Ciella had brought.

"It looks like a dirty stuffed cat." the teacher replied.

Penny, alarmed, said, "No, you have to give that back!"

"Oh, my God, no! That's her emotional support animal. You have to give that back right now!"

The teacher tried protesting, and Penny tried to override her, because that doll has apparently gone everywhere with Ciella since she got it. To doctor's appointments, the hospital, to court for custody hearings, *everywhere.*

Judges and therapists in Ohio know about Sticky, as well as those nurses and doctors, because Ciella won't leave him behind.

Because of all the love and travel, Ciella's Sticky doll is dirty, but she won't let anyone wash it. She's afraid the doll will fall apart, so she won't let anyone touch it, and all some people can see is a dirty stuffed animal, not a well-loved one.

The conversation ended, but after she hung up, Penny received another phone call from Ciella's teacher from the previous year.

"Oh, I'm so glad I caught you," she said. "I've heard about Ciella, and I wanted to let you know we've gotten the situation sorted."

This second teacher had seen Ciella crying during lunch. She pulled Ciella aside and found out what had happened. "Well, tomorrow, you bring Sticky to my classroom. Then, whenever you need a Sticky Hug, you can come over here and get one. Then, you can take him home after school. Will that work?"

Ciella agreed that would work.

At the bottom of Penny's post were a whole series of comments asking whether we could get another doll for Ciella. No, we couldn't. Ciella had actually gotten the last Sticky doll, though I hadn't realized it. Now that I understood just how important those dolls were from that post. I began searching how to get more of them made, but that still didn't help in the meantime.

Penny hopped into her comments, telling everyone that Ciella didn't *want* another doll. She'd asked, and Ciella said, "This doll knows all my fears and secrets. I don't care if he is dirty. I love him with my heart and not my eyes."

I read that, and like years before, with the message from the man in the UK, I cried my eyes out. It blew me away that Sticky meant so much to her. When Mikee found me, I tried reading her the message but I couldn't. I handed her my phone and let her read it for herself.

Further down that same conversation, this person asked, *Well, what does Ciella want?*

The answer was one of the most humbling things I have ever experienced in my life. *She doesn't want a gift. She wants the same thing she wanted for her birthday, which is to meet Chuck.*

To be *that* person to a little one who has had such a rough time is the most incredible and humbling feeling. I know I have used those words a lot in this story, but those are the words that describe so much of all of this. Remember how I had just wanted to give people hope? This. This is what I meant by that. And it feels as good as I thought it would.

Because of Ciella, we produced another batch of dolls for any other people who decided they needed a Sticky Hug. There is also that thing I spoke about Belinda starting, where people send us photos of their Sticky's in different places. That will get to continue because of Ciella. Thank you, Ciella.

The other thing that really touched me is that I found out Ciella refers to me as 'Uncle Chuck.' I've never met her, nor spoken to her on video chat, even. I've written her notes, but mostly, communications happen through her aunt, Pam and Grandma, Penny.

I don't know why or how she began calling me 'Uncle Chuck,' but the fact that she does makes me realize the responsibility I have to her. No, I've never met her personally, but her story is one that we've all heard plenty of times. Life has dealt Ciella all the cards that can make a kid feel like 'nothing'. I know something about that. I can help this one. I can give this one hope. That's all I wanted to do.

There are so many other people that I have met, each with unique and interesting stories in their own right. Each one of those folks has changed my perception of the world in some way. They have each given me a little better understanding of the people I am sharing my little piece of time with.

I didn't even tell you about the people I met, that I know you would know. If I'm honest, the people I have met, that you don't know, make for a far more interesting story than the ones you already do. Each one of those people, famous or not, is someone who I wouldn't have met had I not stopped for that little cat. Do good things, good things come back. Sometimes life it that simple.

7

— • —

YOU ALREADY ARE SOMEONE

Y ou already are someone
    We all want to be someone special, noticed, and important. How this looks is as individual and unique as the people on this earth. When I was young, I thought that being *someone* was all about fame, fortune, screaming fans, and signing autographs.

Man, was I wrong. Those aren't the important things. Those aren't what make you *someone,* or even happy. And those things can disappear in a second. My first round of fame is enough to prove my point.

Do you want to know what makes you someone special?

Kindness. That's what people remember you for. *That's* what makes you *someone.*

Being someone important isn't about what the world does for you or what kind of adoration you get. I don't know how, but that belief seems to be pretty common among many people. I'm going to blame social media again, but I believe that's where many people get it wrong.

It's about what you can do for others, and it doesn't have to be huge. Yes, people like Sumeera and Victor are definitely heroes to me for devoting their lives to helping those kids. Their brand of changing the world is huge. Not everyone is called to that kind of work, though. Not all of us can pull that off. That's okay.

Start small. Smile at the grumpy old man you see at the store. Wave at the mother, taking her kids to the park. Help that elderly lady with her groceries if she needs the help. Just say 'hi' for no reason. Especially in a big city. It's funny to watch people's reactions. We need to say hi, more.

These are the things that make you *someone*. It's really that easy.

Friend, if there's one thing I could do for you, it would be to help you understand that you're *already* someone. It doesn't matter where you come from, who left you when, who didn't love you, or how badly you have been treated. You are now, and have always been, someone of worth.

Your value is in *you*. Not in those people or situations that have let you down. You are worth every bit as much as anyone else on this planet. Everyone is worth something, and that means you, too.

Being famous doesn't make you someone of importance. Anyone can be famous for anything these days. Even finding a kitten. But if you do find yourself with that platform, for the love of God, do something positive for the world with it.

If you can choose to be remembered for lip syncing or changing a kid's life? Pick the second one.

The famous people I admire most are the ones who are also humanitarians, who go to children's hospitals, and set aside time for their fans and those in need. You get to see them being exceptional humans and great examples of kindness. That's why whoever you just thought of as you read that, are loved the way they are. All of those folks have figured out what to do with their fame.

Everyone deserves kindness.

I don't know that I always believed that, but I certainly do now. That's the cool thing about life. We get to learn, and grow and change our understanding of things. You don't have to go your whole life thinking and believing or doing the same things you did when you were younger, or even yesterday.

Now, being kind and showing kindness to everybody doesn't mean laying down and letting folks walk all over you. Grandma showed me that one, too. Okay, two last stories about grandma...

In Southern Texas, 1975, I was riding along with my grandma to take her friend home. Her friend happened to be black. Grandma stopped at an ice cream shop and the three of us went inside. It was a hot summer Texas day, and I was ready for it. I remember they had bubblegum ice cream. It blew my mind. But that's not the important part....

The girl behind the counter was perfectly polite to my grandmother, but with my grandma's friend, the girl was not nearly as cordial. As a child, I didn't know what was happening, but I remember it felt weird.

We were just about to order that beautiful bubblegum ice cream when the girl gave my grandmother's friend a look that must have been the final straw for grandma.

Grandma immediately picked up her purse and grabbed my hand. "Come on. We're not getting anything here."

The girl stared at her as if she couldn't believe someone would change their minds after looking through the ice cream selection for that long. And my 5-year-old little self was crushed. It didn't matter to grandma.

My grandma leaned over towards the girl and, with a big smile, said, "You know, sweetie, you should treat everyone the same. No matter who they are, treat them the same. It'll come back to you."

The way she said it was like she was passing on a big secret to this girl. And, when you look at it, she was. I've met many people over the years, and when people have kindness at their core, even the really nasty people can't seem to be too mean to them. Or maybe it's just that the nastiness didn't bother them as much.

Right after she said that to that girl, we walked away. No bubblegum ice cream and not another word said. No need to hurl insults, scream, or get angry with the girl. Grandma had made her point. The girl probably never forgot her and maybe even learned something. Sometimes standing up for yourself or the ones that need standing up for comes at a price. That time the price was my bubble gum ice cream, but I am proud of grandma for making her stand.

Earlier, I mentioned one of my grandma's favorite sayings was "Bless your heart" (and she really meant it). But she had another one that I may love even more. "What can I do to make your world better?"

Some people will say that they need a fancy car, or a bigger house in order for their worlds to be better, but that's not what is going to do it.

A smile.

A hug.

A kind word on a bad day.

A banana pie for no reason. Yes, even banana pies are kindness.

It turns out those are the things that make the world better for every human, everywhere on the planet.

Sometimes we encounter folks who may have not been shown much kindness. I'm no mathematician, but I'm sure there is a formula somewhere that equates kindness exuded by a person compared to kindness previously received in their lives. They often have a hard shell and when we encounter these people, it can sometimes be tough to find that kindness for them.

Those are the ones that need our kindness the most. If you can show some kindness to someone who is constantly pushing people away, man, you have really achieved someone-ness. Consider it a challenge. How much can you melt that icy heart?

Finding Your People

It's a lot easier to feel like *someone* when we surround ourselves with 'our people'. We all need to find our people, and you also need to know that not everyone is your person, and that's ok.

What do I mean by that?

I've seen people try to be a chameleon, to force themselves to change in order to fit in with a certain group. They'd change how they behaved, how they dressed, and would suppress their own interests—or never gave themselves enough space to figure out what they liked—just to fit in with a group of people.

But the group always knew that one person didn't fit in, so that person would always be on the outside. They felt like no one listened to them, they barely spoke, and when they did, they felt like people would just brush it off. They never felt valued.

That's because that person wasn't with their people.

When you find yourself in that situation, find *your* people. The ones who will support you, who are happy when you're happy, who want you to succeed. Your people are the ones who will listen when you talk and encourage you to share your interests. They want to hear about those interests because they are *your* interest.

The people who are smiling because you're smiling are your people.

My kids have a friend who we'll call Sam. He's very self-conscious about his feet. Especially around the other kids. He has big feet. Not overly big, clown like feet. Just normal big feet. But for whatever reason, he doesn't like them.

I've seen Sam hanging out with a group of kids at the beach, and even on the sand, he had his shoes on. The kids were shouting at him, laughing and asking him why he didn't take his shoes off. He told them he liked having his shoes on. Even on the beach. He dislikes his feet that much.

Then one day he came to our house. I noticed he kicked his shoes off right away and went running barefoot with my boys in the backyard, and that's when it hit me.

Your people are the ones you can take your proverbial shoes off around. Where you aren't afraid of judgment. When you're not embarrassed by your biggest insecurities. When you find that... you have found your people.

I have two groups of people in the world that I feel at home with no matter where I encounter them. Surfers and musicians. I love taking part in both things, but what I really love is the universal language and friendship you find in each of them. I'm sure there are groups like this, for every kind of person in the world, but these two are my people.

Recently, my family and I went to Mexico. There are so many stories I could mention, but this one is the most important. My boys and I were playing in the ocean, along the shore break. Just flopping around in the waves and body surfing right at sunset, and it was the first time my boys had ever experienced warm ocean water. It was a really fun moment for us all.

A little Mexican girl and who I'm guessing were her little brothers, raced down to the water and began playing near us. We're all riding the waves and flopping onto the beach, just having a blast. I speak very little Spanish—enough to be polite—and they had no English, but we're all laughing, smiling, and pointing at the waves. Hand signals were enough to say, *"Okay, you're going? I'm next!"* then, we'd all jump into the waves together. There was so much smiling and laughing, but not an actual word spoken.

You could never have sat us down in a classroom and told us to discuss the color orange. We would have gotten nowhere. But on the water... That's a completely different matter. It doesn't take words to understand someone's smile as they paddle back out after riding a wave.

I know the joy of it, the euphoria of it. They know I understand, and that I'm smiling with them because I'm happy for them and what they just experienced, and because in a few minutes, it'll be my turn.

It's a universal happiness and kindness.

No one is pushing to get ahead. We are all just smiling and laughing and enjoying floating on the water while we wait for our turn.

Music is the same way. I don't need to understand Spanish, Dutch, or French in order to play with someone from those countries. They can grab their guitar, I'll get on the drums... We don't need to know a single word of the same language to have a great time and make something beautiful.

The thing is, though; you have to be open and kind in order to experience those kinds of things. If I was a grumpy old dude and those kids came over, I might have ignored them, or moved away with my own kids, so we didn't have to share our waves. The little local kids would have thought us Americans were mean, and it would have taken the whole beautiful lesson away from my kids. We would have missed that entire experience.

Instead, all of those kids all learned that happiness is universal. We can connect with other people in great new ways using happiness and kindness.

You miss so many cool things in life if you aren't open to experiencing new things. We find so many special moments in life when we just show a little kindness. We also really need to understand that we—none of us, from any culture—are the end all, be all. No one culture is better than another, and we really need to stop judging other people for living different lives.

Before going to Mexico, I was told to be careful and to be on guard. I think everybody who goes to a different country hears those words. I have to tell you that at no time did I feel threatened. Sure, they have their issues, but so do we. The normal, everyday folks down there are so friendly. Like we do, they want to help, to talk, to meet new people. They're just surviving and trying to have a good time in their part of the world, like all the rest of us. They really are beautiful people.

8

CONCLUSION

C onclusion
Short and sweet, right? I wanted to make sure we got to the point, and I'm not one for a lot of words. Say what you need to say and lets get moving, so with that in mind...

I started off this book by saying it wasn't about me. Then I told you a whole lot about me. The point in every one of those stories, about any of those things I have been able to do, was this... If I could do *any* of that... you can certainly do anything you set your mind to doing.

I believed for a good portion of my life that my destiny was to be nothing. I didn't *feel* like I was supposed to be nothing, but somewhere along the line, I truly began to believe life's plan for me was... nothing. To do nothing of any real importance. I wasted a lot of years believing that. You might be too. Don't. You can do *anything* you set your mind to doing. Believe *that*.

I could sum this all up by telling you what you should have gotten out of this story, but that's never been what this journey is about. Everyone gets something different from this story, and that's one of the best things about it. So let me just share some secrets and little life tips with you, that I have learned, and that have meant the most to me...

- Give older folks a minute of your time. It makes a tremendous difference to them, and you never know what kind of cool story you may end up hearing. Just sit and listen for a minute. If you're lucky, you'll be old someday, too. Hopefully, someone will sit and listen to you as well.

- If you see something that needs help, help. It's that simple. That's how we change the world. Reach out a hand, throw out a life ring. Help like it's you that needs the help.

- Never take someone's hope from them. No one ever has the right to take someone's hope. It's often the last and only thing someone has left. Never take someone's hope.

- That being said, never give up your own hope. If you woke up today, there is reason to have hope. Never give up that hope.

- You never know what's going to happen in a day. Keep your eyes open. Magic is all around you, every day. Life is pretty amazing like that. We just have to be paying attention.

- You also never know what someone is going through. Be kind. The biggest smiles can have the saddest hearts and unfortunately, we can't always see that sadness behind those big smiles. If you can't be kind to someone, be gone from them.

- Along those lines, know that asking for help is *strong*. For far too long, our society has pushed the narrative that being brave is 'dealing' with things yourself. You're sad? Perk up. You're upset? Get over it. No, that's wrong. I have talked to so many folks who have lost a loved one who was either too proud or too scared to ask for help. I have lost a couple myself. If you need help, ask. I promise you, your family and friends would much rather help you than miss you. Be brave and ask for that help.

- Stop caring about what the other person is doing. Why do you care who they love? Why do you care who they pray to? Why do you care what their hobby is? If it isn't hurting anyone, stop worrying about it.

- You don't need to be a superhero to change the world. You might make huge, positive changes every day and not even know it. Is there a particular kid you have taken under your wing? That kid may grow up to cure cancer. Your kindness may be the tiny flame that keeps that little mind and heart from freezing over. That's an undercover superhero, my friend.

- Speaking of which... spend some time with kids. If you're an adult, there is a good chance you have forgotten some of the magic of being a child. Blow some bubbles, color some pictures. Make up silly stories and set those dandelions free. Let yourself be a kid. (It's often way more fun than being an adult.)

- Now... if you can't let yourself be a kid, at least let your kids be a kid. Us adults and those kids care about different things. Equally important but wildly different things. Let their things be important too. They really *are* important.

- Slow down a bit, friend. The world we live in wants us to rush. Everything around us is designed to happen fast. To happen right now. The things you are rushing for will still be there. Slow down a bit and enjoy your life.

- Speaking of *that*, remember, life goes fast. It doesn't seem like it when we're young, but I'm here to tell you... life goes fast. Some lives go faster than others. Try to make yours as slow as possible. Savor it. Enjoy it like it's the best Sunday morning cup of coffee you've ever had. Choose the sunset over the tv show. Choose the beach over the housework. You will not regret not vacuuming, but missing that beach trip... Choose the beach.

- The only person who can tell you-you are incapable of making a difference in this world is you. I had a lot going against me and this little cat and I still made a difference. There are lots of folks who had much more going against them than I did. They still made a difference. You can make a difference too. Just go do it.

- This one isn't mine, but I love it... "If you get a chance, take it. If it changes your life, let it." Dr. Seuss. Life is a series of events. Not one long one. You may never get that chance again. Take it. Change is scary, but it's also where you find some of that magic I keep talking about.

- Don't be afraid to be embarrassed. Say something if you have something to say. If you have a 'mission', get going. If you have a dream, go get it. Don't be afraid to be looked at as a fool. Do you know how many 'fools' have reached their dreams because they weren't afraid to be called fools?

- "Never be afraid. Of anything." Grandma.

- "You don't have to do *everything* the hard way." Also, Grandma.

- Love. Love so hard. I hope we get to see each other again, but this may be our only shot. If you love someone, something... anything—love it with everything you have. Love it like you won't get to love it again. Because you may not.

- Forgive. I've spoken to so many people that have such regrets because they lost someone before they could forgive each other. There are very few things in life that are unforgivable. Especially when we are talking about people we love. Forgive. If for no other reason than to free yourself from that anger. You will never regret forgiveness.

- Watch your words. Words are so much more powerful than we realize sometimes. Words alone have caused a lot of pain in this world and sometimes we can't take those words back. Watch your words.

- Don't be afraid to not be everyone's favorite person. Your people are out there. It may take a while and some weird side roads to find them, but they are out there. It's one of those positive things that social media is good for. You'll know your people when you find them. Don't settle. They're out there.

- Make art. Any art. Finger paint, doodle in the dirt with a stick.... I have talked to so many people, from so many places. The happiest people make some kind of art. It doesn't have to be a masterpiece. The cool thing about art is that no one can tell you what is or isn't art. The human soul wants to create. Be happy and make art.

- Throw the ball for your dog. That's all that dog wants in the world. And how easy is that little bit of kindness? Throw the ball.

- I'd also tell you not to be afraid to put yourself out there. Stop the car. Open the door. Be the first one to offer help when it's needed. What are other people going to do? Shout at you? Flip you off? Maybe. But then what? Probably nothing, that's what.

- Smile at strangers. That smile may be the thing that changes their day. Who knows... it may even change their life.

- This one has nothing to do with this story but it has brought a lot of joy to my family and I, as well as the recipient of this small act of kindness and I feel like I need to share it; Secretly, pay for someone's breakfast. It's a terrific way to start someone's day, and it feels great for you, too.

- Talk to people. Ask them about themselves. You

already know about you. Ask people about them. I have had so many incredible conversations with people from so many interesting parts of the world. These conversations have expanded my entire consciousness, and I feel like I understand the world so much better than I did a few years ago. You can always end a conversation if it's going south, but you never know what other directions it may take you in. Talk to folks.

- Ignore the few 'dead flowers'... focus on the field.

- My daughter, who you read about at the beginning of this book, read the first chapter a few days before this book went to print. Seeing her reaction, I felt compelled to come back and make this addition. If you are a young man who finds himself becoming a new father, stick around. No matter what you have to do. When those kids have grown, you will understand why you went through everything you're about to go through. You may not, while it's happening. There will be days you want to quit. Never give up. It will be the best and most important job you will ever have. Be there for those kids, no matter what. And, know you *will* make it, even on the hard days, and it will be worth so much more than you can ever imagine. No matter what else you do, be there.

And finally...

A few weeks after finding Sticky, and after I'd connected with so many people around the world and saw how and where we are all so much more alike than different, I felt like someone had opened this giant book of life's secrets for me.

As if the winds had suddenly parted the fog and I could see what the important stuff really was. It's not our differences. It's the similarities.

It was like a secret door had opened and someone let me take a peek at the next level. Sometimes, I feel like I'm hanging from a ledge by my fingertips, peeking at what we could be. The rest of my body is where we're at, but I'm just able to get my eyes above the ledge to see where we should be, or rather, where we're going. I am happy to say; I have hope, friends.

We all have the ability to change lives and even the world. Every single one of us is important and valuable. We can all make a difference if we decide to live our life with that purpose and what better purpose could there be in this life than to make some smiles and change some lives for the better? That sounds like a beautiful life to me, friends.

I usually say this all started when I pretended to be Roger for that nice old woman. You could also say it started with any of those acts of kindness that were shown to me at any point in this story. Those each made this story happen as well.

I've heard from people of all different religions about their beliefs about how Sticky and I met, and it changes for each one.

As I said earlier, I don't have a calling to a particular religion, so all of them have merit to me. Some might say that God gave me this understanding, or that Buddha showed me a piece of Nirvana. Some say 'the Universe' brought us together, or that it was even just life following its random pattern of chance. They all could be right. I can't say for sure, but man, I'm grateful for the experience.

I've never mentioned this in any interview and to very few people really, but my grandma passed away a few months before I met Sticky. I think this would be exactly the kind of thing she would set up to help me realize I was someone. Something so far out there that I had no choice but to believe it. She told me, herself, over and over and I couldn't believe her. So maybe this was a little, "Ok, let's try it this way then", from the other side.

That's the one I like the most, but I just don't know for sure. All I can tell you is *what* happened.

What happened is that one time, as I was driving down a cold farm road to work, I saw something that needed some help and I was able to help, so I stopped. That one moment changed my life in ways I could never imagine, and it granted me the one wish I had said out loud. To give some folks some hope. I was able to find some closure to some old hurts and man; I have learned a lot about the world. I also got to set off down a really cool road, I never imagined would be open to me. All for being nice for a minute. I am living proof that a moment of kindness is time well spent. With kindness comes happiness, and when you have those two things, you have it all. That's the secret. If I can find those things, you certainly can too. Get out there and find them.

In bringing this to a close, I would tell you this... Believe in you. Even if no one else does. You *are* special. Be kind, be brave, and be yourself; everything else will work itself out.

PS: Hug those peeps!

Made in the USA
Las Vegas, NV
09 December 2022